MOSQUITO VICTORY

Jack Currie

A Goodall paperback
from
Air Data Publications Limited

A Goodall paperback

published by

Air Data Publications Limited
Southside, Manchester Airport,
Wilmslow, Cheshire. SK9 4LL

CONTENTS

1 On the Halifaxes 5

2 You have control... 22

3 Special Flight 37

4 No Green Lights 52

5 Combat Course 75

6 Glider Pilot 92

7 Night Flying on Mosquitoes 111

8 Met Flight to Victory 138

   Glossary 175

I

On to Halifaxes

I always knew I would survive the tour at Wickenby – well, nearly always. And whenever confidence had slipped a bit, it soon came back with six hours' sleep and an egg-and-bacon breakfast. What I did not know was how I should go on surviving, without the Lancaster and without the crew.

It seemed that I had lived for ever with the sound of Merlins in my ears, with Cassidy to navigate, Fairbairn to mind the radio and Walker to nurse the engines, Myring to man the bomb-sight, and Protheroe and Lanham to be the eyes behind my head.

If, on that end-of-tour leave in February, I had hoped to feel relief to have escaped from Wickenby, from the frightening moments and the long, cold hours of waiting to be frightened, I was wrong, for all I felt was loss. As a crew, we had been close enough for each to know, in most circumstances, how the others would behave. We had been mutually critical, but trusting; aware, but tolerant of faults; individualistic to the point of eccentricity, but ultimately cohesive as a team. I felt that they were still my crew, although the tour was over, but to the Air Force they were not. Screened from operations – 'resting' – we were posted every which way, according to our trades.

Fairbairn and Protheroe were sent to a Wellington OTU at Peplow, in wildest Shropshire, to teach their skills respectively to wireless ops and gunners; Myring went to drink saloon bars dry in Lichfield, and to inspire young bomb-aimers at that same OTU where we first met more than a year ago. Lanham, now commissioned, was making life hard for the recruits at Bridgnorth; Bretell, the silent man who had succeeded Lanham in the tail for our last six operations, went back into the Wickenby mists he came from, to fly on as needed, until an armistice or death might end his quest; Cassidy and Walker moved a few miles north-west to the HCU at Blyton and, although my posting should have been another HCU at Lindholme, I joined them there, for Wg Cdr Wood, our first CO on 12 Squadron and my inspiration of those days, was Blyton's Chief Instructor now. 'I expect you chaps would like to stay together,' he grunted, 'though I'm buggered if I know why. I'll fix it with Group.'

I thought of the comforts of the offices and pre-war mess at Lindholme, as compared with the sheds and Nissen huts at Blyton – like Wickenby's or worse – and of nearby Doncaster's delights against those of Gainsborough's grim streets. Then I looked at Cassidy and Walker. The one would be my messmate still, and the other might remain my engineer. I thanked the Wing Commander for the offer and asked what duties he had in mind for me.

'What the hell do you think? Teach the sprogs to fly the Halifax.'

'I don't know the first thing about instructing, Sir.'

'No more do I. Point is, you know a bloody sight more about flying heavies than they do. Anyway, I'll send you on a course.'

No 3 Flying Instructors' School was at a field called Lulsgate Bottom, on the Weston-super-Mare road out of Bristol, and the five-week course – flown on Airspeed Oxfords – was a potted version of the Central Flying School syllabus. The aim, as stated, was to imbue us students with the standard methods of instruction – the correct techniques, the proper patter – but I had an inkling that another purpose was to eradicate the wicked flying habits we were thought to have picked up while flying our tours with Bomber, Fighter or Coastal Command. I had no real argument with the principles of these objectives but, for the most part, I found the process pretty dull.

The Oxford was not an exciting aeroplane to fly, nor yet was it particularly restful. It needed careful handling on take-off and on landing, for the undercarriage was narrow and the little Cheetah engines closely set inboard, and it did not fly itself – as the Anson did – once you were in the air. Furthermore, after 18 months or so of flying the heavies, it seemed ridiculously small, and I felt as a police dog-handler might if asked to exercise a Pekinese.

As room-mate, and co-pilot on the practice training flights, I was glad to have MacLaughlin, that same serene, sleepy-eyed veteran who had been captain on my 'second-dickey' mission to Cologne, the first of my operations in the Lancaster. A minority of that vintage had lived to end a tour, and I had been heartened when MacLaughlin did – not just because I wished him well, but because I reckoned that if he could, so could I.

'What happened to your navigator?' I asked, sitting at the tea-table on our first day at Lulsgate Bottom.

'Tiny? He's with me at Sandtoft, large as life and twice as natural, running the navigation section. Pass the mustard, if you please.'

'And your mid-upper – George Gerrard?'

'Back in Canada, old boy.' He spread great streaks of yellow on his bread and cheese, and chewed contentedly for a while. 'One misses George. Or rather, one misses George and his supply of whisky.'

I tried a little mustard on my own cheese; it did give a semblance of flavour to the pallid stuff. MacLaughlin dipped a biscuit in his tea. 'What's Blyton like?'

'All right I suppose. Jim Cassidy and my engineer are there, and Bill Spiller arrived from Wickenby to take over 'A' Flight a couple of days ago. Woody's CI, of course.'

He took the last slice of bread and margarine. 'Any decent WAAFs?'

'I couldn't say. I don't take much interest in that sort of thing.'

'Balls.'

'There's a Cypher Queen – fair, fat and friendly. And a WAAF Gee – she's the motherly type.'

'How exciting.' He leaned forward, knife poised. 'Don't you want all your cheese?'

It would not be true to say that MacLaughlin and I strained every nerve to do well on the course. He, by nature, eschewed activity of any sort, and I was already plotting a return to operations. From our talks at Blyton, I was sure of Cassidy and Walker: both were game to fly another tour – main force or PFF – provided we flew together as a crew. Lanham, I knew, believed that he had done his share, and was thinking only of the day when he could board the troopship for Australia; Myring had said nothing of his plans, but my feeling was that no more would his bloodshot eye glare down a bombsight over Germany, no more the temperature above the cold North Sea be heated by his curses. I wrote to Fairbairn and George Protheroe at Peplow – both Flight Sergeants now – and they were ready too, on the same terms as Cassidy and Walker. 'Mid-uppers are going back right on six months, anyway,' wrote Protheroe, 'and it'll take you that long to get things organised.'

I would put an application in as soon as I returned to Blyton. Bill Spiller and Woody, my immediate superiors, would surely give their blessing, for old time's sake if nothing else, and if the others simultaneously applied to join me, the P Staff at High Wycombe, remote as they might be, must see the sense and equity of posting us together. A new bomb-aimer and rear gunner had to be recruited – the very situation of a year before, when Myring's and Lanham's predecessors had flown and died with other crews – but that should be no problem. Blyton and Peplow must be full of fellows itching to get back into a Lancaster; I would ask Cassidy to find the one and Protheroe the other.

Meanwhile, the German Air Force was making the best

riposte it could to Bomber Command's campaign against Berlin, now coming to a close as nights drew shorter, and dropped more bombs on London in two months or so than in the whole of 1943. Over a third of these were incendiaries, and my father, while keeping up his Home Guard duties, also resumed his place on the fire-watch roster at Shell-Mex House in the Strand. My mother took exception to the time-fused bombs that came down silently on parachutes and, all in all, regarded the attack as being a graver threat to Whitmore Road than the blitz three years before. She took to sleeping under a Morrison shelter in the dining room, and insisted, when I went home on a 48-hour pass, that I occupy a camp-bed in the same room.

'If the house falls down,' she explained, 'you can pop under here with me.'

'What about Daddy?'

'He's rather silly. He says he likes to sleep in his own bed at night when he's home.'

'So do I, Mummy. It makes a change from listening to MacLaughlin snoring.'

'Nonsense, dear. We're not going to have you do all that bombing just to come home and be hit by a bomb yourself. And you must tell me if I snore.'

In central London, people were seeking shelter in the Underground station passages and platforms, as they had done in the blitz, and it was slightly sobering, when waiting for the last tube back to Harrow after an evening in the West End, to stand among the blanket-shrouded rows of citizens as they settled for the night.

For a while, the Luftwaffe was successful with tactics learned from us – the target-marking flares, the concentrated bomber-stream, the use of radar-jamming – then the defences caught up again, in the way they always did, in my experience. You thought of a great new way to get your bombers to the target, baffle the gunners, fox the fighters, and for a while you had them cold; then they figured out the answer – better radar, different night-fighter control – and they were back on top. That was how it happened in the 'Little Blitz' of 1944: the balance of ascendancy between attacker and defender swung again, and, once the experienced Pathfinder crews had been discouraged or destroyed, the whole thing fizzled out. Back in Berlin, of course, it could have been that the hearts of the German High Command were not entirely in it. They knew that, on the Baltic Coast, their scientists were gestating a brand-new breed of bomber – a bomber with no pilot to discourage and even harder to destroy.

But that unpleasant issue was, as yet, unborn. The moonlit raid on Peenemunde in August '43 – the time when Protheroe was moved to shoot the fighter down – had delayed it for a while.

At Lulsgate, MacLaughlin and I struck up a friendship with two ex-Coastal pilots: debonair, dark-haired fellows both, sharing a sardonic sense of humour. They did not joke, however, when the bomber squadrons flew to Nuremberg at the end of March, and were rather more than decimated by the prowling fighters. They waited for our reaction to that aerial shambles, and to the loss of recent comrades, before offering comment.

'I'll tell you one thing,' said MacLaughlin, 'I'm really rather glad I'm screened.'

'That's nearly a hundred crews gone,' I mused, '700 chaps in one night. I wonder what went wrong.'

'You remember Roden's ghost – at that séance in the farm house? "Stick to navigation", he said. I expect the met winds were duff. Everybody early on target, stooging around…' He made a machine-gun noise with his lips.

'Séance be blowed. Tiny was having us on. You know jolly well it was him tapping the table. He was just making navigation propaganda.'

MacLaughlin's eyes gazed at me opaquely. 'I thought so at the time. But he's always sworn – even when he was sloshed – that it wasn't him. Funnily enough, I'm inclined to believe him.'

We had to tell the story of that firelit room near Wickenby, where May, the farmer's wife, having made some sort of contact with Larry Myring's mother, and been firmly snubbed by George Gerrard's grandfather, had proceeded to invoke the spirit of our late Flight Commander, Squadron Leader Roden. Asked the reason for his failure to return, he answered crossly, 'Blasted flak', and added the advice that was so heartily endorsed (and, thought some, contrived) by Navigator Watson.

At the conclusion of the tale, Pearce said, 'If it's duff forecast winds that get you bomber boys into trouble, I don't see why you don't send a Mossie on ahead to find the winds, and bring them back before you go.'

MacLaughlin nodded. 'What a splendid idea! You don't think that having a Mosquito buzzing over might give Jerry the tiniest clue as to where we were going?'

'It could buzz over several targets – Jerry wouldn't know which the real one was.'

MacLaughlin frowned, and glanced at me. This would not do at all. Ideas about bomber tactics, good as they might seem, could not be entertained from Coastal people.

'Narrows the field though, doesn't it?' I argued. 'They'd only have two or three to worry about, instead of the whole of Europe.'

'Anyway, Mosquitoes operate up over 30,000 feet,' added MacLaughlin, 'or they don't get their range and speed. We're interested in the winds around 20,000.'

'It's very decent of you, Arthur,' I said, 'to interest yourself in our little problems. But I should stick to Liberators, if I were you, and depth charges, and simple stuff like that.'

'That's the trouble with you bomber types,' said Roy Smith, 'You're just like the poor bloody infantry in the last war – over the top when the man says, no thought, no question – it's pathetic, really.'

'Fat chance you'd have,' Pearce joined in, 'of finding a U-boat in mid-Atlantic, or the Med.'

MacLaughlin lit a cigarette. 'No, old boy, we just flatten the factories where the buggers make them. Prevention's better than cure, you know.'

'They're still making them, Mac,' said Smith.

I put down my cup and stood up. 'I can't stay here chattering with you fellows all evening – I've got work to do.'

'What work?' asked MacLaughlin.

'A spot of the old met, funnily enough. Adiabatic lapse-rate, and all that. I've decided that I've never really given it enough thought, and it's going on just above us, all the time.'

MacLaughlin stared at me open-mouthed. 'What an extraordinary idea!' He raised himself from his chair with obvious effort, and put a hand on my shoulder. 'Are you ill?'

'There is an exam in two days' time, you know.'

'So what?'

'Who cares?' asked Pearce.

'Exams aren't for aces like us,' said Smith. 'We don't bother about that kind of thing.'

I buttoned my blouse. 'Please yourselves. I don't intend to fail, and have to do it again.'

MacLaughlin turned to the others. 'It's because he came up through the ranks,' he explained. 'He's never been able to take a gentleman's view – no, that's unkind – the *broader* view of Air Force life.'

Although the last flight of the course was detailed as 'CFI's check', that great man did not stoop so low as actually to fly with me himself, and the duty was performed on his behalf by a Flight Lieutenant – a brisk, bewhiskered man, who seemed determined, during our brief acquaintance, to prove that Training Command pilots could be proper dare-devils, given half a chance. Having permitted me a few moments in which to demonstrate taking-off and leaving the circuit with the associated patter, he took over the controls and employed the next twenty minutes in doing his best to scrape the bottom of the Oxford's fuselage along the chimney pots of all the pubs in Gloucestershire. He continued his demonstration by sub-navigating the suspension bridge at Clifton, carried out a creaking barrel-roll and, with a lordly gesture, indicated that I might undertake the task of flying back to base and landing.

Next day, MacLaughlin and I, with Pearce and Smith, collected our log-books from the Training Wing Adjutant. The results endorsed upon them were identical: 'Assessment as Pilot – average. Assessment as flying instructor – average. Overall assessment – qualified'. It was the first time in 500 hours of flying that I had not been classed 'above average'. Deep in thought, I walked across the tarmac in the gusty morning wind towards the instructors' rest room. The blue sky turned to grey as a shower-cloud swept in from the Bristol Channel and passed across the airfield. I thought of the impenetrable thunderstorm over Hamburg, back in August, that had turned my Lancaster on its back (and nearly turned it inside-out); I thought of the desperate search for Wickenby in November fog, of the overshoot at West Malling on the starboard engines, of the battle with the fighters after Peenemunde, the long, slow, weaving runs across the Ruhr and Mannheim, and the hours in icy cloud to reach Berlin so many times. I thought of all my fellow pilots who had not survived to be instructors: Bob Yell, downed after many hard-fought missions, Alec Richards, Ashburner, Leader-Williams, Belford, Jeffries, Forbes, Yeo, Baxter and many more: worst of all, the dapper Aussie Hutchinson, missing on his 30th and last. If I were an 'average' pilot, what of them?

I found my instructor, spick and span as usual, in a battledress that was better cut than most. He had preserved with me, throughout the course, the sort of wary relationship that a very young schoolmaster might have with a brutish fifth-form pupil. I looked into his innocent, wide eyes, that had never blinked against the sudden, horrid flashes of the night. I saw the smooth, pink cheeks and forehead, unlined by introspective wonderings and well-remembered fear. He smiled politely, waiting for me to speak. But, as I looked, I knew that there was nothing I could say to him. He did not know my story. He had seen the ribbons on my chest, but many men wore those. I had not worked hard to win his favourable opinion, as I had with Wallace Bacon Sheffield and Lieutenant Sena in the States, and at the OTU before I went to Wickenby. To him, I was no more, no less, than an average pilot.

'I came to say goodbye,' I said, 'and thanks for all the gen about instructing.'

'Pleasure, old Currie.' He smiled again. 'I expect you'll forget everything I've told you, once you're back on heavies.'

'No,' I said, 'not everything. You've taught me something I'll remember.'

When the ground-school exam results were pinned up on the notice-board, my name was half-way down the list. Alongside was a sheet of paper bearing the signatures of MacLaughlin, Pearce and Smith. 'Currie – 25th', it read, 'Teacher's pet! Swot!! Toad!!! Bore!!!!'

I flew a late morning detail on the first day back at Blyton and, after lunching in an almost empty dining-hall, looked around for Cassidy in the anteroom. He was not among the usual group of navigators – the Australians Bill Cameron, Noel Knight and company – and I guessed that he had gone back to his hut to write a letter. I picked up a *Daily Mirror* and was casting about for a chair, when his voice rang out across the room. 'Eh, Jack, over here!'

For a moment I stared blankly at the corner where he sat, grinning hugely, between two WAAF officers – one, the podgy blonde I had mentioned to MacLaughlin, the other a girl I had not seen before. This was, I knew at once, a serious departure from the norm. Never for Cassidy the feverish pursuit of womankind that occupied so many airmen in their hours of ease; never would he join Lanham and me in our flirtations, nor Myring in his bar-room conquests. I had an inkling he had met a girl in Ireland once, on leave, for an aunt of his there, sending eggs, had somewhat critically implied as much, but to see him sitting now, waist-deep in women and clearly greatly tickled, was to see apostasy personified. Shocked, I waved a hand and turned away.

A moment later, he was at my side. 'Great to see you, Jack! How was FIS?'

'All right, I suppose. A bit boring.'

'Come on over – that's the new Assistant Adj. Pretty good, eh? I've told her all about you.'

Reluctantly, I put the paper down and followed him across the room. 'Here he is,' he announced, 'my skipper on the Squadron.'

The new girl's eyes were wide-set and merry. She smiled, and gave me an open, friendly gaze; friendly, but appraising – the gaze of a girl who had indeed heard all, if not to say too much, about a man. She had a lot of auburn hair and a beautiful complexion. We talked for a few minutes, once Cassidy had finally satisfied himself that neither one could be in the slightest doubt as to who the other was; and her voice was pleasant to the ear, well-pitched and accentless. It was reminiscent of my mother's voice. On an impulse, I asked her where she came from and, when she replied that she had been raised in Yorkshire, I told her I had, too.

'Jimmy tells me you're a cricketer,' she said.

'Do you play games?'

'Netball, yes, and tennis…'

'And hockey, of course.'

'Why 'of course'?'

'Well, you can't get a commission in the WAAF unless you play hockey, can you?'

'What nonsense!' Few women and, in my experience, fewer WAAF officers laughed so openly and naturally. The blonde WAAF 'G' girl patted her coiffure and picked up her shoulder-bag. They had work to do, she intimated, if Cassidy and I had not. I watched them as they walked briskly from the room. A pretty, games-playing, Yorkshire girl, I mused, with an attractive voice and, despite the all-concealing uniform, an equally attractive and entirely female shape. 'So, Jimmy,' I observed, 'that's what you've been up to while I've been slaving away at FIS!'

'Aw, give a man a chance – she was only posted in the other day. Strange place, strange faces, I was just trying to make her feel at home. You'd have done the same.'

'Not me, pal. I can't afford WAAF officers. They're strictly for the rich colonial troops like you.'

'Don't give us the horrors, Jack, I'm flat, after that leave in Ireland.'

'Have you done any flying, while I've been away?'

'Couple of trips with Des, and one with Errol. I'll fly with you, now you're back.'

'Sure you can spare the time? You don't have to help the Assistant Adj push the paper around, or anything like that?'

'Aw, nuts!'

For the next few weeks I seemed to spend most of my waking hours – and not a little of the rest – in the right-hand seat of a Halifax, trying not to interfere too much with the eager fellows on my left who were teaching themselves to fly the brute. Behind me in the cabin, Walker monosyllabically instructed the pupil engineers and, when the occasional detail took us away from Blyton for bombing or cross-country exercises, Cassidy kept a wary eye on the navigator in the nose compartment.

That was one of the ways in which the Halifax differed from the Lancaster – in the disposition of the crew. In the Lancaster, only the bomb-aimer was stationed forward of the cockpit: in the Halifax, both the navigator and the wireless-op were down there, too. This put a lot more nose in front of you, as pilot, and since, at your back, the cabin top was faired straight into the roof of the fuselage, with no raised 'glass-house' like the Lancaster's, there was a distinct restriction in the field of vision fore and aft. Lieutenant Sena, USAAC,

16

whose constant advice above the training fields of Georgia to 'cultivate the roving eye' still echoed in my memory, would have craned his neck and recognised, with a characteristic snarl, that, in Britain too, some designers did not care whether pilots could see which way they were going or which way they had been.

Comparing the one bomber with the other, you would mark that flattened upper surface, and the longer nose. You would note, too, the squared-off rudders and wing-tips of the Halifax, and the way the tailplane was set higher on the fuselage. It was all solid bulk, the Halifax, all straight lines and angles: the Lancaster's shape was graced by arcs and curves. The vital statistics of length, width and height were very similar – you would need a tape-measure to check that the Halifax was a foot or two longer from nose to tail and from wing-tip to wing-tip, and that it stood a little taller off the ground.

The variations in cockpit layout were more obvious, and few, in my opinion, any kind of an improvement. The throttle-levers, for example, came far less easily to hand – although I liked the friction-lever better, and the trim-tab controls, in contrast with the compact unit of the Lancaster, were all over the place. The undercarriage and flap levers, on the other hand, were much too close together: fumbling for them in the dark, down beside your right thigh, you could be forgiven for mistaking one for the other, and that might make a late overshoot more exciting than it need be. The lever for the bomb-doors was right there with them, but it did not function in the natural sense, as they did, up for up and down for down, and although a tangle over that would not matter on a Lincolnshire bombing range, I imagined it could be an embarrassment over, say, the Wilhelmstrasse. The blind-flying instruments – airspeed indicator, artificial horizon, climb-and-descent indicator, altimeter, gyro compass, turn-and-slip indicator – were in their usual position on the panel in front of you (even Handley Page accepted the standard pattern there), but the other forty-odd dials and gauges were spread around the cabin as though somebody had thrown them in through the window and fitted them wherever they hit.

It would be idle to pretend that, like the Lancaster, the Halifax was a joy, a pilot's dream, to fly. The one seemed always eager to be airborne and never keen to land: the other, to my fancy, was a mite reluctant to take off and fly, and, once you had it in the sky, was only waiting for the moment when you set it on the ground again. Not that it would let you down up there: so long as you flew it, it would fly, solid and dependable, stable and untemperamental. But you had the feeling it was really happier to be taxying quietly back into a comfortable dispersal pan. In a way, this characteristic was a blessing – it was the easiest big aeroplane to land that you could wish for. Persuading the Lancaster to sit down on three points, especially when lightly laden, could be the devil of a job: she would float for miles if you should let her. There was no such problem with the Halifax: all you had to do was put it somewhere near the runway centre-line, chop the throttles, haul back on the stick and down it went, thump, and stayed there.

This trait made it an ideal tool for the job at HCU, of getting pilots used to landing the big, four-engined stuff. It is true that the odd ham-fisted character might burst a tyre from time to time – I even had one who broke the whole starboard undercarriage – but that was all part of the rich pattern of life at Blyton, and at least the Halifax was not inclined to float off the runway's end to land in the back of beyond.

But being a Halifax instructor did not always seem the safest, least demanding, way to earn a living. There were times when I wished I were on my own in a Lancaster, or any aeroplane, far out over Germany, with nothing but fighters, searchlights and flak to think about. The trouble was that, as a new boy, I seemed to get all the Poles to teach: fine, brave, dashing fellows all, and just the lads to have beside you in a cavalry charge, but not, ideally, in a complex, modern aeroplane. Badowski, Fudali, Gratt, Rosochaki, Ostazewski and company were inclined to view the technical details with a fine disdain, to be a little nonchalant about the drills.

As one of these handsome, East European adventurers cruised happily along the downwind leg, only 150 feet or so below the regulation height, I ventured a suggestion. 'Okay, Walewski, how about letting the old wheels down now?'

Whether the wave of his hand was an acknowledgement or a dismissive gesture I could not tell, and I let the matter lie for a few more precious seconds while he gazed about him, humming softly through his nose. 'Undercarriage, Walewski,' I snapped at last, as we neared the crosswind turn.

'Okay, okay.'

The nose fell a little as the wheels unfolded and, quick as a flash, Walewski hauled it up again. The airspeed dropped alarmingly. 'Twenty-six fifty revs might keep us in the air,' I counselled.

With a flowing movement, he thrust the throttles open.

'Revs, Walewski,' I insisted, 'we need more revs, not boost!'

'I know, I know.' He swung gracefully into wind, and pointed the nose at the threshold of the runway like a dive-bomber on target.

'A little flap would help our angle of approach,' I muttered. Walewski's expression was that of a man tired, but tolerant of interruptions. 'If you don't get some flap down,' I predicted, 'you'll never land this thing.' I watched his right hand. 'No, Walewski, flap. The wheels are down.' But by now we were too high, too fast and far too late to land at Blyton. We might have made it into Hemswell, with a squeeze. I told him to take overshoot procedure.

'Is okay,' he drawled. 'I slide in, easy.'

'No, Walewski, this isn't a Gladiator, or whatever you flew last. You don't side-slip Halifaxes. Go round again.'

After a few weeks of this, I began to feel the strain.

Casting aside the cool, impassive patter they had taught at FIS, I hardened up the instructional technique and simply pointed to a dial or lever with the operational word 'speed', 'flaps', 'revs', or, when disaster's face came close, 'I have control'. With some of the more recalcitrant daredevils, I resorted to the simple expedient of administering a sharp blow on the wrist or forearm, to amplify the teaching point I sought to make. I realised that my Lulsgate Bottom mentor would have been unlikely to approve the method, but it proved so effective that soon I was applying it to all my Polish pupils. I received a few strange glances in the pilots' rest room, but the wear and tear on nerves and fibre decreased in direct proportion to the missed approaches.

Nevertheless, I approached the Flight Commander after a month or so, and suggested that I had served my time with the lads from the far side of the Oder-Neisse line and that it would make a pleasant change to fly with an Englishman again, or a Canadian or New Zealander, even an Australian. For all his faults, Bill Spiller was not a totally unreasonable man, and he agreed. I had a few peaceful days with Cornish, Brown or Sutton in the seat beside me, and then I was back on the programme with Badowski and company. I marched into Spiller's little office and glared down at his head, bent wearily over the papers on his desk. The straight, flattened hair was even thinner, and the pale cheeks more lined, than they had been at Wickenby. Looking at him, the memory came back of how he had sent me, for the last two operations of my tour, on consecutive nights to bomb Berlin. 'You've given everyone else an easy ride for their last op,' I had stormed. 'If I get the chop on this one, I'll come back to haunt you, and you'll never have another quiet night's sleep.' And he had smiled, and told me how much better it was to get the thirtieth operation over fast, not to hang about waiting for an easy target and getting the twitch. Perhaps the memory was with him, too, because we grinned at each other when he looked up. 'Yes, Jack?'

'I thought we agreed my Polish period was over – you've put me on with the sods again!'

'Popular request, old boy. I had a deputation in here, asking for you.'

'Balls.'

'Perfectly true. They seem to think you have an empathy with them. "He understands us," they said. I had to take their feelings into account – morale, and all that.'

I got the glare back on my face. 'The hell with them. Listen, Bill, I want to go back on ops.'

'So do I.'

'Seriously. I hate instructing, especially Poles.'

He sighed. 'Put in an application. Through the Adj.'

'I bloody well will.' I turned at the door. 'They use scent, you know – it stinks the kite out.'

'Wear your oxygen mask.'

I threw him a perfunctory salute, and strode out into the sunlight. The door creaked open behind me, and he spoke, a little plaintively, from the threshold. 'No need to slam the door, old boy.'

'Sorry, Bill. Something had to be slammed, and your door was there.'

'That's all right. Incidentally, your second ring's come through. You're a Flight Lieutenant, back-dated to May 1st. Acting, of course.'

I had not expected the promotion, and was duly gratified. From Sergeant Pilot to Flight Lieutenant within the year was certainly no record – pilots on PFF were moving up in half the time – but it was good enough for me. My battledress epaulettes lost that naked look, and my pay went up by two shillings and seven-pence to just over £1 a day. But I was not to be diverted from my purpose by even these rich sops. 'Sir, I have the honour to request,' I wrote, 'that a return to operational duties be approved for myself and the following officers and NCOs of my crew, on whose behalf I am authorised to apply…'

2

You have control...

The Adjutant's office was deserted when I walked in with my application. I pottered for a few moments, catching up on SROs and PORs, until a large, clean sheet of blotting paper on the desk seemed to offer a challenge that no dedicated doodler could refuse. Hitler, Goering and Mickey Mouse answered quickly to a practised hand, and I was well into Winston Churchill when the intercommunicating door with the Station Commander's office opened and the auburn-haired WAAF bustled in, straight-backed and trim, with every button shining like a runway light.

'Hello,' I said, 'where's the Adj?'

'On leave. I'm acting for him. Do you mind if I have my chair?'

'Not at all.'

She sat down and smoothed her skirt. I put the application on the desk in front of her.

'You've drawn all over my new pad!' She gave a peal of laughter and put a hand to her mouth. 'Actually, they're jolly good.'

'Aw, shucks – tain't nothin'.'

'It's frightful cheek,' she said, trying to frown. 'Do you always behave like this in SHQ?'

'Only when I'm sober. Would you put that application through for me?'

She glanced through the text. 'Honestly, I shouldn't think you've got much of a chance. You've only been off four months.'

'How do you know?'

'Jimmy told me.'

'Listen,' I said, and stared into the amber, emerald-flecked eyes, 'we're never going to win the war if I don't go back on ops. If you don't see that application through, you're playing right into Jerry's hands. Have you got a bicycle?'

'Yes, if some aircrew bod hasn't pinched it again. Why?'

'There's a little pub at Owston Ferry. It's a nice ride through the lanes. I'll pick you up at six o'clock.'

That evening, I washed the dark marks of the oxygen-mask off my face, brushed my hair and set off for the WAAF site. Cassidy, cycling towards the hut with his colleagues from the Navigation Section, hurried after me. 'What's on, Jack, where you going?'

'Oh, just for a little exercise. Down to the river, maybe.'

'Whizzo – I'll come with you.'

'Might have a couple of beers at The Ferry.'

'That's okay, I'll have a lime juice.'

I frowned. 'I don't really need you, you know. I can navigate myself that far.'

'Yeah,' he cackled, 'but what about coming back?'

Knight and Cameron, I noticed, had fallen in behind. I revealed my secret.

'Ah, good on you, Jack,' he cried, 'I knew you two would get along.' Over his shoulder, he passed the news to his companions, and we cycled on together - they more happily than I.

Half an hour later, we propped our cycles beside the bank and rang the bell for the ferryman. The pub was a rambling place, oak-beamed, low-ceilinged and hospitable. Over the beer, relaxed and comfortable, I looked round as we talked to the Australians in their deep-blue uniforms; at Bill Cameron's close-cropped, greying hair and thoughtful eyes; at burly Noel Knight, whose sun-creased cheeks and brow-shaded glance spoke of the farmer he had been; at Cassidy, with that pale, good-tempered face I knew so well. I turned from their strong features to the full-lipped, fresh-complexioned girl, and her steady, amber eyes smiled back at me.

For a while the talk was of Australia, of Brisbane's beaches, the friendly streets of Sydney, the endless rolling plains where Noel bred his sheep, then of the Melbourne Cricket Ground, of how Bowes had bowled out Bradman, how McCabe confronted Larwood in his prime. And of tennis, which we vowed to play together, since the Station, for all of its privations, boasted two grass courts. Time passed, and the bombers, climbing out of Elsham Wolds, Killingholme and Kirmington, began to fill the sky with sound – enough to make a window rattle in its ageing mortar. Cassidy it was who voiced the query in our minds. 'I wonder where they're going tonight.'

'French target, for a dollar,' said Cameron. 'They mostly are, these days.'

'Yeah, and they were only counting a third of an op,' Knight added. 'The blokes at Binbrook were really going crook about it when we were over there, eh, Bill?'

'Were they ever!'

'Then they went to - waddya call it - Mailly-le-Camp...'

'And lost 42, out of three-fifty odd.'

'And after that Command scrubbed around the idea, and they counted a full op.'

He rose to his feet, towering above the table, and asked the WAAF if she would have something more to drink. No, she would make her whisky-and-orange last, but he and Cameron had more rum and I another beer. Cassidy, venturing a second glass of lime-juice, mused on. 'A third of an op – cripes, that'd be 60 for a second tour.'

'Who cares?'' I countered, brave with bitter. 'Better than flogging the circuit here. Anyway, you can't back out now – the application's in.' I turned to the girl for confirmation.

'I was checking up,' she said, 'and you can't apply for other people to be posted – only for yourself. Sorry to talk shop, but you brought it up.'

'No, that's okay – we'll all apply. I'll get word to the others.'

'I'll be in it,' said Cassidy, 'but don't count on them all being soft targets when we get back. Wouldn't you know it'll be the big city and all points east by then.'

'That'll be up to Ike,' said Cameron. 'The bombers have to go where he says now. The Yanks are in charge, Jim, everywhere - Eisenhower here, MacArthur back in Aussie.'

We had to agree this was so. After all, they had the manpower, money and materials. 'Yeah, but what a bunch of drongoes,' Knight observed, 'down the smoke they're everywhere, loaded with money, sheilas on both arms...'

He turned to the WAAF for her opinion of our allies.

'Not much, from what I've seen,' she replied, and smiled. 'I prefer Australians – and Yorkshiremen. Not,' she added, to the chorus of approval, 'that I want to give you any wrong ideas – I'm practically engaged to a Scotsman.'

We could not approve of that. Scotsmen, we warned, were tight-fisted barbarians with strange passions for porridge-oats and bagpipes, who treated women shamefully. As she laughed, I watched her thoughtfully, and wondered what she meant by "practically".

The system was that the pilot-instructors of Flight Lieutenant rank took it in turn to act as officer in charge of flying – 'OC Day' or 'OC Night' for short – whenever the Halifaxes were in the air. They were meant to give advice, if it were needed, to the control staff in the tower on pilots' problems, and to make decisions on the fitness of the weather, as to cloud-base and visibility, or as to shifts of wind that made a change of runway necessary.

It was a wonderful June morning when half-a-dozen of us were sprawled upon the grass in front of Spiller's office, watching the aircraft come and go, and desultorily discussing Operation Overlord between remarking what a smooth landing that was, what a shaky take-off that. One, indeed, was a very shaky take-off: the aircraft went into a nasty, split-arsed turn at 300 feet or so, and lurched on round the circuit like a drunken cripple with a heavy list to port.

Watching this, it came to me that something nasty was about to happen. 'I don't quite like the look of that,' I said. 'Who's OC Day?'

'You are,' croaked Spiller through the window. 'I wish you people would read Orders.'

I reached the tower like a nervous batsman getting away from the bowling, and took the steps two at a time. The control officer was frowning through the window when I reached his side. 'It's a pupil,' he said, and told me the name. 'On first detail after solo.'

I held out my hand for the microphone. 'Starling Queenie, this is Woolsack. Are you in any kind of trouble?'

The amplifier in the tower broke silence as the pilot thumbed his transmit button in the cockpit, and the sound of people shouting at each other filled the room. The Halifax roared on around the field, now straightening a little and gaining a few feet of precious altitude, now banking steeper and slipping down the sky again. I tried the microphone a second time, and through the babel caught the one word - 'ailerons'.

That this held a signficance for me was because I had once experienced a problem with the ailerons myself. In the titanic thunderstorm that had saved Hamburg – already fearfully assailed - from a fourth attack last August, my Lancaster had been seized by ice and so tossed by the seething air-base that both ailerons were torn off in recovering from a spin. By rare luck and - so Lanham always said - the hand of God, that aircraft had flown back across the sea and landed safely at Wickenby, and in the process taught me how to manage without lateral control.

But this pilot, now fighting for his life, was not in quite that case. His Halifax still had its ailerons, for I could see them, but it seemed that either they were jammed or, for whatever reason, would not answer to the wheel. 'Shut up and listen,' I said into the microphone. 'Straighten up with your engines, then climb and sort yourself out.'

I said this very slow and clear, and I said it several times, but I might have saved my breath. The men in the cabin of that aeroplane, panting, cursing, shouting, were beyond my reach or help. I looked at the control officer. Already he had warned all other Blyton aircraft to keep clear of the circuit: now he rang a summons for the fire-truck and the ambulance. Halfway round another horrid circuit, the Halifax at last ran out of sky. It hit the ground with cataclysmic violence, just beyond the boundary on the far side of the field. A towering column of black smoke showed the firemen and the doctor where to go, but, except for an empty rear gun turret, debris was all they found.

Next day, when a party of technicians were collecting bits and pieces, the control column wheel was discovered, and with it the reason why the aeroplane had been so hard to fly. When the Halifaxes were not in use, standing in dispersal, their control surfaces could be damaged by being blown about in the wind. To prevent this happening, the ground crews would put locks on the controls inside the aircraft and, normally, would take them out for a flight. But if the wind were high or gusty, they would leave the locks in for the aircrew to remove. In either case, it was the duty of the pilot to make sure they were removed by someone. The aileron lock, painted red and anchored by a split-pin, consisted of two arms which clamped the pilot's wheel, or 'spectacles', for that described its shape, against the column. This lock, though damaged by repeated heavy blows from - the technicians judged - the cabin fire-axe, was still in place.

So charred and mangled was the evidence, you could not tell whether the red paint had ever been there, and clearly the crew had never found the split-pin, but how anyone could set an aeroplane in motion from dispersal, let alone commit to the air, without at least a gentle waggle of the wheel - 'test controls for full and free movement' was what we taught - was incomprehensible, and yet it must have happened. 'Inexcusable' said the experts, shaking their heads, but I could not help thinking of those last few frantic moments when that pilot realised he had made his last mistake.

A diversion came a few days later, when a gleaming, brand-new Spitfire purred over the field, with that unmistakable whistle of the wind across its wings. It made a close, right-hand circuit and settled smoothly on the grass beside the runway. Sitting at a table in the crew-room, writing up my week's flying hours from the Flight Authorisation Book, I watched idly through the windows as it weaved a zig-zag path towards the visitors' dispersal by the watch-tower, and swung round on one wheel to face the wind. I was about to turn back to my log-book when the cockpit canopy slid open and the pilot, clad in clean, white overalls, stepped on to the wing and, pulling off a leather helmet, revealed a head of shoulder-length, blonde hair.

Appreciative gasps and whistles broke out in the crew-room. 'All right, you chaps,' I said, 'I'll handle this. She's probably lost – you carry on with your work.'

Sauntering out to the dispersal, I was passed in the first 20 yards by a ravening pack of aircrew, and contented myself by affecting to inspect the aircraft while they clustered around the pilot. She was a tall, slender girl, pale-faced, with bold, blue eyes, an aquiline nose and a determined little chin. You would have thought she was about 18. Her name was Joan Cunnington, she was saying, based at White Waltham with the Air Transport Auxiliary, and she had been ferrying the Spitfire from Cosford to somewhere up in Scotland.

I pushed through the pack and picked up her flight-bag. 'I'm the ATA liaison officer. Will you come with me, please?'

Leaving the dogs to prowl, muttering, around the Spitfire, I led her decorously away. 'ATA liaison officer?' she commented, 'I've never heard of that before.'

'It's a fairly new appointment. Excuse me for asking, but were you lost, or anything like that?'

'Only very slightly. The main problem was petrol – do you think I could get some here?'

'I'm sure we have a gallon or two around the place somewhere.'

'I think it likes 100 octane best – but whatever you've got will do. And there's a red light that came on a little while ago – would it be anything to do with oil pressure?'

When she had booked in at Flying Control and the servicing had been arranged, I suggested a pre-luncheon drink in the Mess. Cassidy, Cameron and the Assistant Adjutant joined us in the bar, and the talk was all of aeroplanes. Most of her flying had been on the Swordfish and the Barracuda, and not a lot on Spitfires. I asked her why she had made her circuit to the right, and she fluttered golden eyelashes. 'I haven't practised turning left yet.'

I thought I had seen through this camouflage of feminine helplessness - for the ATA's sake I certainly hoped I had – but Cassidy's eyes were wide with wonder. 'You mean... but, cripes, what happens if you get off track to starboard?'

'I try not to, you see. I try and keep a bit to the left all the time.'

'Yeah, but...' His eyes flickered to me, and I looked back at him without expression. 'But, supposing you did...?'

She sipped her gin and tonic. 'I'd just have to go somewhere else, wouldn't I?'

'Aw, not necessarily,' said Cameron, with admirable gravity, 'you could keep turning right until you came back on to your course to steer.'

'Wizard idea! I must remember that.'

Cassidy chuckled. 'Good on yer, Bill. Hey, why don't we remuster to the ATA? I reckon they could use a couple of good navigators.'

It was time for an aircraft captain's authority to be asserted. 'How would you like,' I asked, 'to fly a Halifax?'

I had her immediate and total attention. 'Gosh – rather!'

'As my second pilot, of course. I'm doing an air test after lunch.'

Walker's eyes seemed ready to depart their sockets when

I helped the white-overalled, blonde vision into the left-hand seat of JD 313 that afternoon. Standing behind me as I took the dual seat, he lifted the ear-flap of my helmet.

'Eh, Jack,' he muttered, 'You're not letting her take it off, are you?'

'Why not? What's the matter, do you want to live for ever?'

'No, but another tomorrow would be nice. This thing's had an engine change.'

'Stop panicking. I'll take it off – the lady can hold the pole when we've got some height.' I turned on the intercom and the engine master cocks. 'Ground-flight switch on "ground", Johnny. One and two tanks on.'

We started up the Merlins between us, and shirt-sleeved riggers, bending under the whirling shadows of the prop-blades with long-practised care, pulled the heavy chocks to either side. A sergeant, pacing backwards, led the way out through the hardware on the pan. His parting grin, with thumbs raised high, might have marked the pleasure that he took in seeing another piece of Tech. Wing plumbing leave the line, or in my second pilot's pretty face – or both.

'It's a long way from the ground up here,' said Joan, 'about three Spitfires high…'

We lumbered round the peritrack and pulled up at the caravan. I locked the brakes and intoned the pre-flight drill: 'Elevator trim – two points back …' (The rudder and aileron trims were on the port side of the cockpit – Joan checked them neutral.) '…Pitch fully fine, flaps – one third, supercharger – 'M' gear, air intake – cold, rad. shutters – auto. Okay, Johnny?'

I pressed the transmit button. 'Woolsack, Starling Baker. Take-off – over.'

'Baker, you're clear to take-off – over.'

'Baker.'

To say that I enjoyed taking off (or landing, for that matter) from the right-hand seat would not be strictly true.

Not that it was all that difficult – not so hard as trying to bat or bowl left-handed – just rather awkward, like shooting a rifle with the butt in the wrong shoulder, with your wrong eye looking down the sights. But, probably because it was so awkward, you tended to concentrate harder on it, and the results were sometimes reasonably smooth.

I climbed to 25,000 feet, below a layer of broken stratus, and set the trims for straight and level flight at 160 mph on the ASI. 'Okay,' I said, 'You have control. Just fly it like a Spitfire, but with both hands, both feet and a bit more muscle. It won't react so fast.'

The Halifax was such a stable aircraft that, if you trimmed it right, you could raise or lower the nose, let go, and it would gradually porpoise its own way back to level flight, more or less at the height you started at. Similarly with the ailerons and rudders, no matter what you did, it would slowly wallow its way straight again. It was, in fact, the ideal aeroplane to go to sleep in. Joan, of course, had no idea of going to sleep: she was living every moment, in command of the placid monster. She managed the level flying and gentle turns with no trouble at all: her only difficulty came in trying to hold the nose up when the banking angle steepened and she had no spare hands, or did not think, to use the elevator trim.

We climbed into the layer of cloud, and flirted with the tops that billowed round the Halifax like breaking waves of vapour. The cabin windows showed a kaleidoscope of grey, white, whiter-than-white and blue. Apart from flying very low, it was the only sort of flight that gave you the idea of speed: up high, and in the clear, it was as though the land and sea rolled slowly back beneath you, while you hung there suspended, static, in the sky.

Taking the controls, I gained another thousand feet, cut the fuel to both the outer engines and the starboard inner, and feathered each propellor in its turn. I gave full-boost and revs to the labouring port inner, and told Joan to wind on rudder trim to counteract the yaw. 'You have control,' I said. 'Take it straight down through the cloud. You can shoot a terrific line at White Waltham about flying a Halibag on one.'

I did not mention that straight down was the only way that it would go in that condition. Below the cloud, and sensing Walker's disapproval hissing coldly on my neck (stopping and starting Merlins was, to him, a task for engineers to undertake), I put the engines back in business, and flew south along the Trent until we reached the railway line that ran from Retford into Lincoln. We followed that when it turned north-east for Market Rasen, past Fiskerton and Wickenby – which I pointed out as the bomber base – then west across the fields, past Faldingworth and Hemswell, back to Blyton.

'Woolsack, this is Starling Baker, rejoining, over.'

'Baker, you're clear to rejoin. Runway 29, Queenie Nan Howe one-zero-zero-two, two aircraft in circuit. Call downwind, over.'

'Baker wilco.' I asked Joan if she would like to take it in, but she smiled and shook her head. 'Perhaps when I've taken the Charles Atlas course.'

'Okay, I have control. Check brakes off, undercarriage going down, 'M' gear, cold air, rad shutters open, twenty-six fifty revs, thirty degrees of flap. Woolsack, Baker downwind, over.'

'Baker, you're clear to finals. One ahead.'

I let the speed come back to 140 mph, and swung on to the crosswind leg when the chequered runway caravan came level with Joan's shoulder. Another steady left-hand turn took Baker on to the approach, with the full flap coming down and the ASI needle creeping back to 110. The Halifax ahead was touching down: if it did not burst a tyre, the timing was all right. 'Baker, finals, over.'

'Baker, continue.'

I made the last checks for the landing: pitch fully fine; undercarriage lights all green. 'It's a longer approach than you're used to,' I said, as Joan peered through her window.

'I was wondering where the airfield was.'

'Twelve o'clock low – you'll see it when I put the full flap down.'

'Baker, you're clear to land, over,' said Woolsack.

I greased in on all three wheels, like a snowflake falling onto water.

'Let me know when we're down,' said Joan.

There was no doubt about it: having a pretty girl alongside was a great incentive to flying right. I was saying as much in the Mess a few days later: 'They ought to be on issue, along with the 'chute and the Mae West. When I go back on ops...'

Woody interrupted. 'What makes you think you're going back on ops? You've only been here five minutes.'

'My application, sir, no one could resist it.'

'Applying's one thing – posting's another. Anyway, you'll have to get in the queue – I've been here longer than you have.'

I stared at him. Erect enough, but developing a noticeable paunch beneath the belt of his battle-dress; dark moustached, but I suspected that the reason he had the hair around his temples shaved was to conceal the fact that he was greying. He must have been getting on for 30 years of age, and I had never thought of him as a rival for a place in a bomber cockpit. 'Come on, sir, you've done two tours already. And, with respect, don't you think you're getting a bit past it?'

'Cheeky young bugger,' he snorted. 'Put him on OC Night for a week, will you, Spiller?'

Group Captain Nelson had joined in with the guffaws at my impertinent remark; now he cleared his throat to speak, and silence fell. It tended to do that in the Mess, when the Station Commander had something to impart. 'I'm glad you're keen on flying with women, Currie, because I've got a little job for you tomorrow.'

'Your merest whim is my command, sir.'

As COs went, I took a good view of Eric Nelson. He was

no glass-eating, fire-breathing hell-raiser, like Basil Crummy at Wickenby, but he was a patently decent, pleasant man, who carried his responsibilities and rank as to the manner born. Furthermore, I had proof that he did not think ill of me – at least, not as a pilot – for he had chosen me to take his younger brother flying when that fine fellow, a paratrooper captain home on leave from Burma, had called on him at Blyton. 'Show him what the Halifax can do,' the Group Captain had said, 'Make him sit up a bit.' With that carte blanche, for 40 minutes I had put LW 336 through its clumsy paces, mostly at ten feet or so above the waters of the Trent, and even Ivor Nelson, brave man that he was (for you did not wear the red beret, let alone command a Gurkha company in action, if you were short of nerve) turned a little pale beneath the even tan, to the evident content of brother Eric when he met us on the tarmac after landing.

'I'd like you to fly my Assistant Adj. to London in the Oxbox. She's posted to the Air House, on this new Flying Bomb Directorate, and they want her urgently.'

I believed I knew just how they felt. My feelings for the girl had developed a degree of warmth over the last few weeks, and the social scene at Blyton had seemed to offer promise of something more than flying talk and ale. The trouble was that she, before commissioning, had been a radar plotter in Fighter Command, and sufficiently well-thought-of to be snatched, with three similarly qualified young women, by this new unit when the V1 bombs began to fall, and the Air Ministry set to work on seeking out their launching ramps. So both their Airships and I needed Section Officer Irene Ninette Gracie, and they had just that little bit more pull.

'She'll be right, Jack,' said Cassidy, 'I've gotta call to make at Aussie House. I'll come down with you – give Nina a hand with her bags – and Noel Knight'll be in it too, to navigate you back.'

As ill luck would have it, the air was tubulent on 23rd June, with an occlusion lying in a long diagonal across the Oxford's track to Hornchurch which, at 15 miles east of central London, was the nearest I could get my passenger to Whitehall. After ten minutes of bouncing, lurching flight, a glance behind me showed a pale, unhappy face beneath the auburn curls, and a tiny handkerchief pressed to the lips that had been so sweet to taste the night before.

No use expecting Cassidy to help, for he was suffering as much as she. He, of course, had always known air-sickness: so long as he had been an airman, his stomach had betrayed his heart. That he had flown on through the years, and never failed, was one of the traits that bound me to him. Nor was Noel, at the navigation table, looking in his usual rude health. I beckoned Nina to the dual seat beside me, and raised my voice above the Cheetah's busy roar. 'Keep it straight and level for me, while I check the travelling 700.'

Her eyes grew even rounder with alarm. 'I don't think…'

'You can steer a boat – it's just like that. Pick a point on the horizon, straight ahead, and try to keep it at the same place in the window. Go on, there's nothing to it.'

She tucked the handkerchief inside her sleeve and, very straight, set her feet upon the pedals and her hands upon the wheel. I affected to scrutinise the log, and hid the hand with which I kept the aircraft on its rocking course. There was a story at that time about a man who, planning to take a girl upon an ocean liner cruise, went into a chemist's shop. 'Four packets of Durex,' he ordered, 'and a bottle of seasick pills.' The chemist packaged the items with a frown. 'I can't understand why you guys do it if you know it makes you sick.' It was the antithesis of this on which I based my simple remedy: if you are the guy who is actually doing it, whatever it may be, it does not make you sick. Only passengers get carsick, not the driver; you never meet an agoraphobic farmer, nor a claustrophobic miner.

In this case, anyway, the theory worked. Nausea forgotten, the lady steered the ship as though Butch Harris, Charles Portal, Sir Archibald Sinclair, and Churchill himself, depended on her. After a while, she became self-confident enough to unglue her eyes from the horizon and flash a glance across the cabin. 'Oh, you cheat,' she cried, 'you're flying it yourself all the time!'

'No, I'm not. It's all yours – I just have to keep my thumb near the radio button.'

'Oh.' She reverted to that point in the distance, but suspicion had entered her pretty head. 'Why?'

I thought of saying, 'If we get struck by lightning, or both engines catch fire, or we're attacked by a squadron of Messerschmitts, I want to tell the world about it,' but my good angel told me to unthink that. 'Normal flight procedure,' I said, 'there's no button on your wheel.' We covered the 140 miles to Hornchurch in exactly 60 minutes, but they told us not to join the circuit straight away. 'Orbit Angels Three,' said Flying Control, 'we have a red alert.'

I did not see or hear the flying bomb coming, only the flash and bang as it landed on the railway line that ran beside the field. Cassidy's face appeared between the passenger's and mine. 'Cripes, what was that? Someone pranged?'

'One of Nina's doodle-bugs, giving her a welcome.'

Hornchurch told me I was clear to join. I made a gentle landing and began to taxi back towards the tower. 'Visiting Oxford, hold your position, over,' said Control.

'Oxford Wilco. What's up now?'

'Another hostile in the circuit.'

We saw this one go over, stub-winged and tiny, with the rocket engine flaming on its back. When it had passed, steady on course for London, I set the passengers down at the transit pan. Knight secured the door, and I watched them walk away, Cassidy smiling, carrying the cases, Nina walking briskly, erect and trim. She stopped once, turned and waved, looking very small there on the open tarmac, and my heart seemed to falter like the engine of the doodle-bug. I shook myself and called control.

'You're clear to taxi – call me for take-off clearance, over.'

I released the brakes and took the throttles in my hand. 'Okay, Noel, let's you and me get back to Blyton, where it's safe.'

3

Special Flight

'They've turned it down flat, old boy,' said Spiller, 'not a hope. Your gunner and wireless-op could probably get back on a squadron, and your engineer, in their turn. Even Jim Cassidy...'

'But we want to go back as a crew, Bill, the way we were at Wickenby. That's the whole point.'

'Sorry, old boy. You're a QFI now, and you've got to do your stint. That's the way it is.'

'Oh, Christ!'

'Never mind Christ. Look, pilots are queuing up for miles to get on Lancs – chaps who've been on training jobs for years, chaps from desk jobs, not to mention all the sprogs from flying schools. There's a hell of a lot of chaps ahead of you.'

I always seemed to be glaring at Spiller about something, and it had as much effect as throwing snowballs at a tank; nevertheless, I glared. 'You're bullshitting me. Rolly Stewart went back last week, and he's only been screened three months.'

He pushed a packet of Players across the desk. 'Rolly was no bloody use as an instructor, that's why. Good bloke, and all that, but...'

'He wasn't any worse than I am. I've told you before, I loathe it.'

'That's not the way I see it, Jack. As a matter of fact...' He lit my cigarette with a lighter made from a cannon-shell. '...they've asked for you at Sandtoft. They're opening up a special flight there, to train instructors – a sort of heavy FIS.'

'I don't want to go to Sandtoft. It's even worse than this place – I've seen it from the air. And MacLaughlin told me...'

'I hate to be blunt, Jack, but the war isn't really about what you want or don't want. Anyway, you ought to be jolly bucked – they've only picked four of you, from all the HCUs. It's a real pat on the back.'

'More of a kick in the arse, I reckon.'

In the air that afternoon, I was thinking about what he had said, and trying to reconcile myself to the prospect of the posting, when a loud report and a tearing rush of air disturbed my thoughts. I was flying from the left-hand seat, with my pupil, one Flying Officer Mulrooney, on his first familiarisation detail, beside me. Mick Mulrooney, a raw-boned, ginger-headed Irishman, had been one of the few RAF instructors with the US Army Air Corps when I was a cadet there, in the States. He had been friendly and free with me then, and when chance brought him to Blyton with his newly-formed crew, I had arranged that I should be the one to see him safely through the course. That, at least, was the intention, but now it seemed that his first experience of the Halifax would not be totally encouraging.

'Bloody hell,' exclaimed Mulrooney's mid-upper gunner, 'something just bloody missed my bloody head!' I could barely hear him, for the wind was sucking the helmet, with the earphones in it, off my head. I pulled the chin-strap tight as he cleared his throat and rephrased the report. 'Captain from mid-upper. An unidentified object has passed close to the turret, travelling aft.'

'It's all right, mid-upper,' I told him, glancing up at the open sky, 'the pilot's escape hatch went. Perhaps you or the rear-gunner could see where it lands – I'll swing a wing.'

Mulrooney flicked his mike-switch. 'Is it supposed to do that?'

'Oh, yes. Little pieces are always breaking off Halifaxes. You'll get used to it.'

I noticed that, being a conscientious pilot, he was wearing goggles on his forehead and, as a minor duststorm was being stirred up in the cabin, I was glad to borrow them.

'Captain from mid-upper,' said the sergeant gunner, now back in control of his emotions, 'I can see the hatch going down – it's shining in the sun. If you hold the bank, I'll try and get a fix on where it falls.'

In the evening, Mulrooney and I drove to the farmhouse nearest to the gunner's pinpoint. Mulrooney's tour of duty in the States had accustomed him to a way of life which dictated that everyone, from officers to the guy who swung the propellers on the flight-line, must own at least one motor-car, and he had therefore invested, on returning to embattled Britain with a dollar or two saved, in a second-hand Morris Ten, thus becoming the only officer at Blyton, apart from Squadron Leaders and above (who had the use of Service cars), to be mobile on four wheels.

The barely damaged hatch had been discovered by one of the many Italian prisoners-of-war who, not ungrateful to have escaped from the unfriendlier North African environment, now tilled the fields of Lincolnshire, and it awaited our collection in an outhouse. 'Might've landed on one of my beasts, that might,' said the farmer, 'or on my nut, for the matter of that. Could've done us a mischief, couldn't it?'

We had to admit that it could, and promised to be more careful in the future.

'Never mind more careful,' said the farmer, and his ruddy cheeks creased as he grinned. 'Just make sure my old woman's out there next time, and aim it accurate-like.'

It was the end of June, and the cornfields basked in the still-burning sun as Mulrooney drove the Morris homeward on the long, straight lanes. He stopped at the little inn at Corringham, and persuaded the gaunt landlady to produce some Irish whiskey. We reminisced about the days at Cochran Field, the Vultee basic trainers and the pleasures of down-town Macon, and then turned to the future. 'What's it really like,' he asked, sipping a second glass of Jameson's, 'over the target – all the flak and so on?'

'You'll find out soon enough. You've been a featherbedded flier far too long – it's time you joined the league of frightened men.'

He brushed a finger each way over the gingery bristle of moustache. 'A Mulrooney knows no fear. In any case, it can't be all that bad, or you wouldn't have got through.'

'That's quite a different matter,' I said, 'I'm an ace.'

'Ah, yes, to be sure.'

'Actually, it *isn't* all that bad, Mick. Not the barrage flak, anyway. You just have to ignore it. But if your rear-gunner tells you that it's sort of creeping up behind you, that'll be predicted flak, and you want to get out of the way.'

'How?'

'Alter course and height right smartly. I'll show you tomorrow – that and the evasive action for fighters. You and your gunners ought to practise it as often as you can, with the Spits from Kirton Lindsey – we call it fighter affiliation.'

As we drove back to Blyton, I told him about my rejected application for another Lancaster tour, and of the Sandtoft posting. 'I'm going next week – I shan't be able to see you through the course.'

He parked the car behind the Mess, and we walked through the long shadows of the hedges to our Nissen huts. He asked if I had thought about Mosquitoes. 'Some of the screened pilots and navs at OTU were putting in for the Light Night Striking Force – apparently it's being expanded. You might stand a better chance of getting back on Mossies. They say its a super airplane.'

'Maybe it is,' I growled, 'but the Lancaster's the Queen.'

The train took me as far as Ealand, but no bus would run to Sandtoft until 10 o'clock. The pub was an oasis in a desert of silent, scattered houses. I dumped my baggage in the hallway, bought beer and sandwiches, and settled down to wait. It turned out that my choice had fallen, either by luck or instinct, on the Sandtoft aircrew bar – every community near an airfield had one – for the bar-room soon began to fill with flying men.

Beer was earnestly consumed, and the buzz of conversation grew in volume as though deafness was endemic. Dimly-remembered faces loomed through the smoke of many cigarettes. 'I'm pretty sure we met at Lindholme – weren't you with Joe Muntz?' 'Don't you remember Frosty's end-of-tour binge at the Snake-Pit? It was me that put you in the taxi – me and Wally. He got the chop on Leipzig, poor old sod, did you know?'

The evening wore on agreeably enough but, to my mind, the social quality was much enhanced when the door opened and a pretty, blonde woman, wearing a green twinset and a pair of rare silk stockings, squeezed into our midst. All the stools and chairs were occupied – one of them by me – and, although most of the fellows gave some sort of greeting, no one made a move. Chivalry personified, I offered her my knee. This she cheerfully accepted, throwing a casual arm about my shoulders and enveloping me in the heady odour of powder, scented soap and just a hint of whisky. There seemed to be nothing else to do with my left hand – the right was holding a glass of beer that somebody had bought – than to put it round her waist and, so occupied, I had every confidence that the time until the bus was due would pass without the slightest pain.

The lady's buttocks wobbled gently on my thigh. 'Sure I'm not too heavy for you?'

'Good heavens, no. I'll tell you when to change knees.' I drew my arm a little tighter and decided that our situation called for an exchange of names.

'Mine's Blanche,' she said, 'but everybody calls me Blondie.'

'Do you work at the airfield?'

'Not exactly work – I sort of live there.'

As we chatted, poor old Wally's friend began the chorus of a squadron song, and Muntz's crewman refilled my glass with beer. A bewhiskered bomb-aimer sang his verse while balancing a pint-pot on his head. The door opened again and two more officers came in. I regarded them casually over Blondie's shoulder: the one, an unwinged Flight Lieutenant whose world-weary face and First War campaign medal ribbons proclaimed the Adjutant; the other a bulky, grey-haired man with four rings on his sleeve. Those nearest to the door drew to a semblance of attention, with a murmur of 'Good evening, sir.' Clearly the Officer Commanding Sandtoft, I decided, and gave him a cheerful smile, sure that, in the circumstances, he would excuse me the formality of rising to my feet. Surprisingly, he looked back at me with the sort of expression that a man might wear on discovering the source of the nasty smell on the landing. Blondie turned her handsome head and beamed at him. 'Hello, darling,' she cried, 'you're just in time to buy a round.'

Later – and it seemed much later – I remonstrated with the people in the bus. 'Why the hell,' I asked them, 'didn't one of you bastards tell me she was the CO's wife?'

'For one thing,' a voice replied out of the darkness, 'we're not exactly sure she is.'

'And for another,' said a second voice, 'you didn't give us much of a chance.'

'At least he'll remember you,' Wally's friend consoled me, 'I've been here a year and he still calls me Jones.'

'You think he ought to know your Christian name?'

'No, but my name's Kershaw.'

That I never seemed, thereafter, to establish a rapport with that Group Captain did not surprise me, nor did it really matter much, for within the month he had been posted and replaced by Basil Crummy, whose command of Wickenby had run, at last, its famous course. My relationship with him was well-established and generally cordial in nature, resembling in most respects that of a medieval tyrant and favoured slave. Crummy was an autocrat, but he had the style to match. He was a despot, but his despotism worked. I liked him. And he brought with him Colin Tapley, an ex-movie actor, who had been in charge of flying control at Wickenby throughout the time that I was there. Here was a man whose bearing was as noble, and his manner as distinguished, as his capacity for beer, and he made a welcome acquisition to the Sandtoft social scene.

I did not, however, hit it off so well with my new Flight Commander, one Squadron Leader Marshall, an immensely keen man, clean-cut, crisp curly-haired, with an accent as curiously clipped as a low comedian's impersonation of the archetypal officer. A far cry from the easy-going, quietly spoken Spiller, was the hyper-efficient Marshall. So pleased was he, so obviously gratified, to have command of this elite instructors' flight, that I should have known it would be hurtful when I told him, on first meeting, of my immediate intention to seek a posting somewhere else.

'Ai dain't knai whethah you realaise it, Curreh, but you're jolleh luckeh to be a membah of this Flaight. We are gaying to raise the level of flaying throughout the whaile of the Command. Ai should forget about Mosquitays if Ai were you.'

That night, the operator said that I was through to London, and I pressed the button A. 'Is that the WAAFery?'

'This,' said Primrose 6121, a little stiffly, 'is the St. John's Wood WAAF Officers' Hostel. To whom did you wish to speak?'

The warm, clear voice came on the line.

'Hallo,' I said, 'is that the whom to which I wish to speak to?'

'Hello, Jack. Have you been drinking?'

'Only alcohol. How are you?'

She was well, but did not care much for the Air Ministry. After station life, the place seemed like a prison. People there were pasty-faced and tired, bad-tempered. 'Not surprising, really - there's quite a row going on by day and night. Oh, I wish I were back there with you this evening, cycling down to the pub with you and Jimmy.'

'The hell with Jimmy. Anyway, I'm not there now. I'm at...' The operator interrupted: time was up and I was out of shillings. 'I'll write you about it, Nina.'

'Yes, you jolly well do. Just leave the bar early for once and write me a nice, long letter.'

There was quite a lot to write about, once I set myself to do it. About what a salubrious place was Sandtoft, three strips of concrete and a camp of corrugated iron, set in the flat, green midst of nowhere; about how wearyingly eager was my flight commander, how sycophantic my superhuman colleague pilots; about how unvaryingly undelicious was the food, how bleak my hutted quarters. Better news was that elsewhere on the base, doing the routine HCU instruction, were such old friends as Watson and MacLaughlin, and Mugsey Johnson, the laconic Londoner who had been beside me all the way from Air Crew Reception Centre back in the Spring of 1941, through the Arnold scheme in Georgia and the Shropshire AFU, until we went our ways to different Squadrons – he to 101 at Ludford Magna, I to 12 at Wickenby. Furthermore, I scribbled on the flimsy Mess notepaper, I had my application in to fly Mosquitoes and, given half a chance, would win the war for her in no time flat. In conclusion, I confessed that I missed having her around, counselled her to take no wooden nickels and to keep her head down when the buzz bombs came to town.

Two or three times most days I clambered into the cabin of a Halifax and took some HCU instructor through the drill. Everybody had to learn the FIS-type patter and procedures, as amended to suit the heavy bomber and my flight commander's whim. Take-offs and landings, overshoots on four engines and on three, steep turns, stalls and asymmetric flying – it was a grinding, unadventurous routine. I put it all across with tongue in cheek, especially when the pilot I was teaching was an old chum, like Johnson, Rowland, the Australians Wellham (whom I had raced home to Wickenby from Berlin so many times) and Errol Magnus, and the Canadian Dave Tribe, all of whom knew every bit as much about the game as I. Being the men they were, they accepted the experience of being *in statu pupilari* with equanimity and a better grace than I would have been likely to command, and went through the drills with conscientiousness and skill.

Sometimes, with a pilot I knew well, I liked to end a detail with a mind-unwinding burst of low flying along the Trent, or hopping hedges on the great expanse of farmland, where the POWs would look up from their harvesting and duck, or run for cover in a ditch. Beautifully stable and steady at low level, the Halifax was perfect for this sort of nonsense and, despite the fact that Nina ended very letter with instructions not to do it, I nurtured still the name that I had gained way back in Georgia (and paid for hard with 50 hours' pack drill) of being the lowest-flying fool in the business.

Another diversion in those summer days of 1944 was cricket: knock-up matches on the camp and more serious engagements when Basil Crummy detailed me and Carey, the New Zealander, who could bat a bit, to play for whatever team attracted his patrician interest at the time. It was his style to toss me the new ball, set three slips and two gulleys, with himself at a ridiculous mid-off, and demand immediate results. Woe betide me if the top few batsmen were not back in the pavilion before I was relegated, panting, to long leg.

We played against the Lincolnshire XI on the steelworks ground in Scunthorpe, where the pitch had been maintained so flat and true that even Harold Larwood would have been hard put to it to make the ball bounce much above knee-high – very different from the track at Doncaster, where you could rap the batsman's knuckles from a length. Nevertheless, I did not disgrace myself entirely, our batsmen made the most of the conditions, and Crummy's disposition was redolent of sweetness and light in Appleby-Frodingham's social club that evening. His moustache approached my ear. 'Lend me a quid, Currie, there's a good chap. I'd like to buy these fellows a drink, and I seem to have left my wallet.'

'That's what you said at Gainsborough,' I muttered, 'you still owe me one from there.'

'Don't quibble, man. The value of this sort of fixture can't be measured in terms of the odd quid.' He snatched the note from my reluctant hand. 'Let me know when it reaches a fiver, and I'll give you a cheque.'

A stout, bespectacled man, with a silver watch-chain on his waistcoat, came to our table, and beamed benevolently at Crummy. 'Excuse me for asking, but have I the pleasure of addressing Mr Edwards?'

Crummy shook his head. 'This is Group Captain Edwards,' he said, and indicated the big Australian beside us. Hughie Edwards, VC, DSO, DFC, was CO at Binbrook, where 460 Squadron lived, and no mean cricketer, despite a damaged leg which warranted a runner to assist him at the crease but which did not, I had observed with interest, prevent him trotting up a ten-yard run to bowl.

The stout man introduced himself. He was the honorary secretary, he revealed, of the social club, and greatly honoured to have so notable a flier on the premises. It would be more than his position was worth to let the opportunity pass of persuading the Group Captain to step on to the stage and say a few words. 'The lads,' he said, embracing with a gesture the snooker, darts and cards players, and the plain old-fashioned drinkers, who had joined the cricketers, 'would really appreciate it.'

Edwards laughed, and shook his head. 'No bloody fear. You'll get no speeches out of me, old boy. Sit down and have a grog.'

Crummy put a hand on the stout man's arm. 'Group Captain Edwards is joking. Of course, he'll be pleased to do as you ask, as soon as he's finished his drink.'

'I meant it, Basil,' protested Edwards, as the beaming secretary departed, 'I couldn't make a speech to save my life. You do it.'

'Nonsense, Hugh. You must.' Removing the cigarettes from a Players packet, he pencilled a couple of sentences on the flattened cardboard and pushed it along the table. 'That ought to meet the occasion.'

Edwards limped across the floor and mounted the stage, a handsome figure in the much be-medalled tunic, with a boyish lock of hair falling across the forehead of his pleasant face. Reading, with knit brows, from the packet, he mumbled Crummy's words. 'Splendid, cricket — holds Empire together — well-known hospitality of steelmen — salt of the earth — airmen rely on them — keep up the good work — war as good as won.' Mopping his face with a handkerchief, he returned to the table amid a hearty burst of clapping and expressions of goodwill. Crummy gave him a wolfish grin. 'There you are Hugh – no trouble at all. My packet, please.'

Crummy was less pleased a few days later, when I answered his accustomed summons with the news that I had a 48 hour pass and meant to go to London. 'Nonsense, Currie,' he bleated imperiously, 'we're playing the police!'

'It hurts me like anything to let you down, sir, but I do like to see my people occasionally. And forty-eights are hard to come by here.' I did not care to tell him that I would be spending one whole day with Nina, snatching her away from Whitehall and taking her on a tour of my old haunts. The programme was for morning coffee with my mother, lunch at The King's Head on Harrow Hill, tea at The Old Millstream in Amersham, and back to Pinner in the evening for drinks in The Queen's Head bar with John and Paul, the Braund twins, schoolday friends and fellow-cadets in Georgia, now on leave from their Halifax base in North Yorkshire.

It turned out to be that rare occasion when the plans all worked out well. Even the buzz bombs that flew over Nelson's sand-bagged column passed on harmlessly to westward while we waited, tensely holding hands. Sun shone, birds sang, everything and everyone was charming. The Braunds, unchanged by time, commissioned status or the bomber-pilot's life, were as charming in their differing ways as they had been since we were in short trousers. Nina, paler than at Blyton but prettier than ever, charmed them in turn, charmed my mother, and all day enchanted me. It was a happy time.

She told me about the Scotsman who, it seemed, had soberly courted her for years: whether the feelings that she had for him were grounds enough for marrying, she was not entirely sure, but a sort of understanding had developed that, sometime, they would. All that, I thought, was nothing to do with me. She was here, and now, and everything was charming. I stood in the corridor all the way back to Yorkshire and did not mind at all.

But back at Sandtoft was a badness. Mugsey Johnson, with – for once – no grin on his good-natured face, was the one to break the news. 'There were these two details yesterday morning, Butch…' (the men with whom I learned to fly still called me by that curious nickname). '…Mac was down for fighter affil, and me for three-engined landings and overshoots. Well, old Mac never did like anything too violent, you know that, and he asked us to swop. I said okay, and he goes off with the pupe for the three-engined detail. The circuit was pretty full here, and apparently he decided to use the Trent as a runway for the overshoots. I found all this out later, see, when I landed. Nobody seems to know what went wrong, but they found them on the straight bit, north of Owston Ferry, pranged on the bank.'

It was one of Johnson's tricks to produce an exaggerated, but realistic, gulping noise as humorous reaction to some unwelcome piece of news. He did this now, or something close to it, but with a chill around my guts I knew he was not joking. 'They were all dead, Butch –killed on impact. Mac was in the right-hand seat and listen, this is the bit I can't bloody well understand, they said his eyes were closed when they found him. Yeah, and he had a book, you know, a novel in his hand.'

Never mind that, I thought, that could not matter less. MacLaughlin had his little ways. He would have shown the pupil how to make the overshoot on three, and then let him get on with it. He would have relaxed there in the sunshine burning through the perspex, just as he relaxed when the searchlights felt for him above Berlin, Frankfurt and the Ruhr, and when he came back with the Lancaster full of holes and two engines out of action from Turin. Just as he relaxed when the flak-shells burst around him on Cologne and I, beside him in the cockpit on that second-dickey trip, sat tense and apprehensive. Thirty times he had flown serenely back to Wickenby from the target, against the odds, and now a clumsy pupil, on a July day in Lincolnshire, had brought him down.

'Old Mac,' said Johnson, groping in his blouse pocket for a cigarette. 'It's a bugger, isn't it?'

At Wickenby it had been a commonplace event to take the pre-flight supper with a friend, never to set eyes on him again. Here at Sandtoft, it seemed outrageous, tragic and somehow absurd. Of course I knew that people died in training: seven of my classmates had, in a Georgia thunderstorm, Dave Garrett had, trapped in the cockpit of a burning Oxford, Charlie Davidson had crashed. And there had been the crew at Blyton, in the control-locked Halifax, and many more besides. But MacLaughlin?

'Yes, it's a bugger all right, Mugsey.'

The only thing for it was a wake, and Watson, MacLaughlin's mighty navigator, must attend, as a sort of surrogate next-of-kin. 'Right,' he said, when I put it to him, 'but not in the mess. I don't fancy a lot of chaps who didn't really know him slobbering over old Mac. We'll go to t'pub.'

Private cars were not so rare at Sandtoft as at Blyton, and even Johnson ran an aged Austin Seven. Colin Tapley, who had known MacLaughlin well at Wickenby, squeezed in with us, and we took the northward lanes that ran through Crowle to Eastoft, where a tavern called The River Don offered the simple comforts that we sought. The landlord had several pretty daughters, no shortages of beer, an understanding with the village constable and, best of all, bed and breakfast for those times when the thought of a return to Sandtoft with a giggling Johnson at the wheel would make the boldest blench.

Nor was petrol any problem: when Johnson's coupons were exhausted, the landlord's brother Albert – a beaming, round-eyed farming man who doubled as the village comic rascal – had a private pump. He also harboured the delusion that, as motors needed petrol, so did flying men need whisky and, should you refuse his offer, you were liable to find that any carelessly-attended glass was copiously laced. Although, now free of Lanham's constant censure, I was less abstemious than at Wickenby, I was not a whisky pilot yet, and, if Albert had not been the landlord's relative and such a cheerful, guileless sort of villain, I would have thrown his headache-mixture over him and let his petrol-pump go hang. Instead, I took the prudent line, and poured it into the urinal's gutter, with regret for such a sinful waste of ale.

So, with darts and dominoes, while Johnson made sheeps' eyes at the eldest daughter and Albert told his esoteric village tales, the evening passed. 'How's things going with that lass of yours, then?' asked Watson, sitting heavily on the bench beside me and giving me his steady, policeman's gaze.

'Who do you mean?'

'The WAAF at Blyton, man. How many have you got?'

'She's not my lass, Tiny. I only wish she were. Matter of fact, I got a letter this morning. Her Scotsman's there, on embarkation leave, and they're painting the town, in between the buzz bombs.' I glowered into my beer. 'Lucky bastard. I wouldn't be surprised if they get hitched up before he goes.'

'How does that suit you?'

'It doesn't suit me at all.'

He banged a great fist down on the table, and the glasses bounced. 'Well, don't just bloody sit there – do something!'

'Like what?'

'Ring her up, you dosey sod. Tell her you love her, for Christ's sake.'

I stared into the broad, strong face, the pale blue eyes intense, the hairless eyebrows wrinkled in friendly exasperation, and thought about his words. The landlord, listening, was wiping glasses at the bar. 'He's right, Jack. You're like to lose her, else.' He jerked his head towards the private room. 'Go on, you'd best use my phone.'

It took an age to find her in the hostel. When I did, she said, 'I'll bet you're in a pub.'

'I've been talking to Tiny Watson. He said I ought to ring you.'

'Oh? Actually, I rang you about an hour ago. A Newzealander called Carey answered – thought the Tannoy was calling him. He sounded so nice, and it was lovely to talk to an old bomber type again. He said you'd gone out somewhere.'

'How's your haggis-basher?'

'Who? Oh, yes. He's all right. As a matter of fact, he's asked me to marry him.'

'Don't do that, Nina.'

There was a short pause on the line from Primrose 6121.

'Why not, Jack?'

'Because…' Watson's words were in my head, my mouth refused to say them. They seemed such a confession of unmanly weakness. But Watson was not weakly, not unmanly, and he had said them simply. 'Because I love you, damn it, Nina.'

'Oh, well. That's nice to hear.'

'I'll have to ring off now – that was the second lot of pips.'

'Goodbye, darling. Oh, and Jack…'

'Yes?'

'Give my love to Tiny.'

4

No Green Lights...

The Halifax was vibrating so much that a gang of navvies with pneumatic drills might have been at work in both the wings. The detail with Ned Kelly was completed, anyway, but I landed, taxied back and took off again, just to see if I could make the shaking stop. Sometimes, if the wheels were spinning in their housing when they were retracted, there could be a certain resonance within the aircraft, but although I braked the wheels before retraction, the pneumatic drills were right back on the job. Indeed, the higher revs for take-off seemed to make them work the harder. 'I don't know what's the matter with this aeroplane,' I chattered through my teeth, 'but it's certainly got a bad case of the shakes.'

'Yeah,' said Kelly, 'it's shaking as much as those Eyeties did when you beat them up. You reckon we mighta hit something?'

'I didn't notice anything, Ned, but you could be right. We'll check.'

I put the quivering monster down again and stopped it on the taxiway. 'Hop out, Johnny, and take a look around. There could be a POW hanging on the tail-wheel.'

Walker made a slow perambulation of the aircraft, the radio-lead dangling from his helmet, the crotch-straps of his harness hoisting his trousers high above the ankles. His long face was expressionless as he crawled back up the fuselage and took his place behind me. He pushed his RT plug into its socket and turned the mike-switch on his mask. 'I can't see much wrong,' he drawled, 'except that we've got square-tipped prop-blades on the port side, and there's some kind of foliage growing out of the air-intakes.'

When I scrambled down the ladder in D Flight's dispersal, the sergeant fitter was staring at the damage and moving his greasy forage cap to and fro to scratch his head. I grabbed him by the arm. 'Get all that greenery cleared out of there, Chiefy, and disappear it, or I'll be for the high jump.'

'How did you manage to do it, sir?'

'I think I must have flown through a tree.'

He picked up a sprig that had fallen from the engine. 'More like a hedge, I'd say, sir. That's hawthorn, that is.'

'Never mind what it is, Chiefy, get rid of it. Between you and me, I was laughing so much at the time that I didn't actually notice.'

'I can clean the intakes up all right, sir, but what about the prop blades? There's a good three inches off of them.'

I had already thought of that, and decided on a story. 'I shall say I hit a flock of birds, and you can say that's what I told you.'

In the mess at lunch-time, the Flight Commander's reaction was entirely satisfactory. 'Bai jove,' he exclaimed, 'jolleh nasteh, birds. Same thing happened to me once, in Indiah, aild boy. One ectualeh came right through the windscreen. Let me get you a spot of something.'

Less propitious was that afternoon's development, when an ammunition box, stuffed with leafy debris, arrived on Marshall's desk, with a note from the Chief Technical Officer. 'F/Lt Currie may have flown through a flock of birds,' it read, 'but apparently they were building a nest at the time.' Marshall's expression, when he could bring himself to look at me, was that of a man to whom the full significance of the story about a fellow nourishing a viper in his bosom had been suddenly revealed.

I was bad news so far as OC 'D' Flight was concerned, and I was having my share of bad news, too. McLeod was dead, I heard – handsome black-haired Mac – and Scotty Walker, of the Glasgow urchin's face and caustic wisecracks. They, with Garrett, Featonby and Johnson, had been my good companions on the way to Wickenby; from the days at ACRC Regent's Park, the Stratford ITW, the Ansty Grading School and the US Army Air Force. Worst news of all, the Braunds were gone, within a few days of each other, as close in death as they had been in life.

Marshall, for his part, could get rid of his bad news, and promptly did, by arranging my transfer to B Flight: I could not escape from mine so easily. In fact, for the first time in five years of war, I began to brood about it, and I found the perfect place for brooding on the far side of the camp. There, the back door of the tiny inn, the Plough, abutted on the airfield boundary, while its front door faced the public road. As deputy B Flight Commander (my transfer had been something of a back-handed advancement), I had acquired a Service motor-cycle, strictly for use within the airfield which, it could not be denied, embraced the Plough's back door. I had a late evening flying detail, but so what? A couple of beers and a good brood was what I needed, and drink and brood I would.

I sat at a bench beside the open window of the back-room bar, listening to the birdsong and the far whine of a petrol bowser on the peritrack. The beer was flat. Hamlet, I remembered, had complained about the beer being flat. Stale, flat and unprofitable, he had termed it. Or maybe it was life he had been talking about. He had talked a great deal about life, if it came to that. Death was really the subject of my brooding: there seemed to be too much of it about. And it was happening to all the wrong people – all the good guys. You could not afford to lose all those good guys, like MacLaughlin, like Mac and Scotty, and Dave Garrett, and Charlie Davidson, and Hutchinson – on his last trip, for Christ's sake – and John and Paul. Particularly John and Paul.

I livened up the beer with a tot of whisky. It still tasted flat, but not so stale. No, the world was going to suffer for the loss of men like them. Never mind the world – let it suffer. It deserved to. What about the parents of the twins, down there in Pinner? Vivid, laughing mother; proud, handsome father – the twins had been the jewel in their ring of life.

I asked the barmaid for a piece of paper and another whisky. A couple of airfield contractor's men and a farmworker or two were grimly addressing themselves to beer and dominoes. 'Dear Mr and Mrs Braund,' I wrote, 'I was terribly sorry to hear about John and Paul...' I stared out of the window. As a sentiment, it seemed inadequate: as a statement, quite redundant. Why would they want to know that I was sorry? They had enough sorrow of their own, without me telling them of mine. I poured the whisky into the unprofitable beer and drank it, thinking of last January, when the twins had come home from their tours of duty as instructors in the States and I, too, had a break before my last two operations. John had come to Wickenby and sweated it out beside me for the last week of his leave. He had begged to be my second pilot on one of the Berlin raids but, accepting the official refusal with good grace, had been content to fly with me on NFTs, and was cheerfully supportive when Cassidy and I stumbled into the cold Nissen hut in the morning's early hours.

It must be bad enough for parents to lose one son, but two... Nor did they need me to tell them that. I screwed the paper up and tossed it through the window. The light was on the fade. 'For everything there's a season,' I muttered, 'a time for every purpose under heaven. A time to be born and a time to die...' Your twenty-third year could never be the time to die, whatever purpose heaven had ordained.

'A time to plant and a time to pluck,' growled a man at the domino table. 'That's in Bible, that is. Is that right, mister?' He turned to his companions. 'You buggers didn't know that, did you? Aye, a time to plant and a time to pluck.'

It seemed to me that I rode the Royal Enfield round the peritrack with tremendous flair, although once or twice I had a little trouble with the gears. 'Excuse me, sir,' said the pupil pilot, when I joined him at dispersal with his crew, 'aren't you taking a parachute?'

'No, sergeant. I've decided I'm not going to jump out of this aeroplane tonight. You're not going to jump out, are you?'

'Well, no, sir-but…'

'That's all right then. Let's get the thing in the air.'

I got it in the air all right, and climbed it straight ahead. I did not want to bother with all that traffic-pattern stuff: changing all the revs and boost was such a bore and, anyway, I could not read the gauges very well. There was a fine, white, winking star up there, and I held my course on that. After a while the pupil started muttering, and I told him to speak up.

'I said, are we going on oxygen, sir?'

'Oxygen?'

'Yes, sir.'

I considered his suggestion. I had nothing against oxygen. In fact, I liked it. I liked the smell of it. Not only that, but it was known as a necessity of life. On the other hand, you should not just turn it on for fun. There were, quite properly, constraints upon its use. In daytime, you would normally breathe it in above 10,000 feet; at night some time before you reached that altitude. It was true that we were flying at night – that was one point in the pupil's favour – but what about the height? Unfortunately, the altimeter dial seemed rather blurred from where I sat. 'What altitude,' I put to him, 'should you start using oxygen at, then, sergeant?'

'Ground level, sir, if we knew we were going above 10,000 feet.'

'And what height are we now?'

'Eleven thousand, four hundred and fifty feet, sir.'

'Eleven thousand…?'

'Four hundred and, well, sixty now, sir.'

'In that case, you've answered your own question. Turn it on immediately.'

He fidgeted about a bit. 'Do you think you could turn it on, sir? The control's just in front of you, and I can't reach it without undoing my harness and my 'chute.'

Clearly the chap was something of a chatterbox, but he had a point. Actually, I found the knob quite easily, considering how dark it was, but no sooner had I turned it than the aeroplane yawed to starboard. The relationship between the cause and the effect, surprising though it seemed, was clear, and to turn the oxygen back to 'off' was clear; the work of but a moment. Still the nose swung to the right.

The voice in my earphones startled me. 'I think we've got an overspeeding prop on the port outer.'

'Who said that?'

'Me, sir - the engineer.'

'Let's try and use RT procedure, engineer.'

'Yes, sir. Flight-engineer to Captain, I think we've got...'

'All right, I heard you the first time.' You found that sometimes. Chattering was infectious: the whole crew had caught it from the pilot. Nevertheless, the engineer was right: the needle on the left-hand rev counter was swinging round alarmingly. Not only could I distinguish that, but suddenly I was feeling rather cold and unelated. I turned the oxygen on again and feathered the port outer. 'Okay, sergeant, we've lost an engine. What's the procedure?'

'Take emergency action and continue with the detail if possible, sir.'

'Right. Remind me what the detail was.'

'Circuits, landings and overshoots, sir.'

'Then what are we doing up here at 11,000 feet?' I had him stumped there: he could only mumble something to the effect that he had been wondering about that himself. 'I suggest you take this aircraft back to base, sergeant, rejoin the circuit and show me a really nice three-engined landing. You have control.'

I slumped back in the seat, and felt in my pocket for a piece of chewing-gum – not just because the motion of the jaws would keep the ears clear on descent but because my mouth was tasting like the bottom of a birdcage and my sinuses like passages for fumes of alcohol. I watched the pupil's actions carefully. For all his chattering, he seemed to know his stuff: zero boost, 2000 revs, a steady turn on to his navigator's course and a gentle, powered descent. All went well until the downwind leg, when he selected 'Undercarriage down. That's funny,' he said, 'No green lights.'

'Probably the bulbs. Pull the dimmer knob – it brings on the spares.'

He did that: still no greens. 'Sure you've got the lever down,' I asked, 'not in neutral?'

He made sure. 'Okay,' I said, 'bring the throttles back a minute.'

The warning horn blared through the cabin. 'Shit,' I said. 'Engineer, check the locks are out.'

I knew that I had spoken, but there was no sound to prove it in my earphones. I checked my mike-switch – it was on. I checked my plug and socket – properly connected. I turned and beckoned to the engineer. Pulling aside his helmet, I shouted in his ear. 'Can you hear me on the intercom?'

Reeling slightly from my breath, he shouted back. 'The last thing I heard anybody say was "shit", sir.'

It is in emergency that you really need communication: shouts and gestures, written messages read by lamplight, are not the ideal media for passing information and instructions. A further complication was that, on three engines, I did not want to lower the wheels until I knew that we could land and, as we could not talk to flying control, nor it to us, this was no easy matter to arrange. Nevertheless, after a lot of flying around in circles, and some expenditure of Very lights and perspiration (especially by the engineer, who had to pump the wheels down), we got the brute down on the runway. It was just two hours and fifteen minutes since I had steered the nose at lofty Rigel, and I made two resolutions, both of which (one, admittedly, some years later) I kept. First, that I would henceforth follow Lanham's dictum and 'never mix flying and grog'; second, that if I should ever meet Sir Frederick

Handley Page, I would speak my mind about his Halifax.

At Wickenby, meanwhile, Rory the artistic gunner, still engaged on a protracted second tour, had at last succeeded in cajoling, wheedling and bullying a motley group of airmen and airwomen to take part in a play. 'They've sent me a couple of tickets, of course,' said Crummy. 'You can come with me. I'll be leaving at half-past six.'

Sweetened by a glass or two of gin in the well-remembered Mess (although there were few remembered faces there), we lounged in the front row of the Station cinema and let Rory and company unfold to us 'The Case of the Frightened Lady'. Harshly lit, occasionally inaudible, nevertheless the play swept on with verve and some dramatic impact. Rory himself, and his current boon companion (a tall, young Irishman with a darkly handsome face), in the leading roles, carried the less gifted members of the cast along with them. Only now and again I heard the sound of a Merlin engine, far out on the airfield, as it cleared its throat to sing, and my mind's eye left the players on the stage, and turned back to a scene six months before, when the seven of us spent an evening in that cinema, trying to concentrate on 'Casablanca', while we waited for a postponed take-off to Berlin, for the final operation of our tour. Then we had sat close to an exit at the back, in case we should be called for: Cassidy beside me, Walker dreaming, open-mouthed, Protheroe vocally appreciative of Ingrid Bergmann, Fairbairn hushing him and passing cigarettes, Bretell a watchful statue, Myring fast asleep.

'Jolly good show, Rory,' I assured the beaming actor when the play was ended, 'and you were awfully good yourself.'

Beads of sweat were breaking through his mask of grease and powder as he took me by the hand. 'It's sweet of you to say so, Jack dear, and it's lovely to see you.'

The Irish consort hovered near, a wary expression on his petulant, proud face. 'And Terry, you were super, too,' I added hastily, 'I can't understand why Denham haven't snapped you up.' Nor need you concern yourself, my jealous friend (I mentally continued), I am no threat to your relationship with Rory, no matter with what warmth he holds my hand – my propensity is not towards our sex. Quite, in fact, the opposite – towards the singularly unfrightened lady who wrote nonchalantly from London about the doodle-bugs' effects.

In the hostel, she and her room-mate, Mary, had on numerous occasions taken refuge underneath their beds, the blackout boards had blown off the windows and, at eight o'clock one morning, the breakfasters had gone to ground beneath the tables – an exercise which cost a ladder in a precious pair of stockings. A nearby block of flats was hit with the loss of many lives, but they were pressing on regardless at the Ministry, under the direction of a wooden-legged Wing Commander with a broken back, who looked like Boris Karloff in one of his more scary roles.

'She is so natural and unaffected,' I confided to my mother in a letter, 'and yet always interesting. I never feel I have to amuse her or flatter her, and we seem to spend most of the time laughing at each other. She thinks I'm the most conceited fellow she has ever met – my self-confidence appals her. I think she would be a wonderful wife. In fact, if I had any money I'd marry her now.'

At my mother's instigation, Nina and Mary moved from NW8 to a boarding house on Harrow Hill. Although they had to make an earlier start to catch the tube at Harrow 'Met', their nights were quieter. One morning, having overslept, they arrived at twenty minutes to ten, and found themselves trotting up the Air House steps behind the Chief of Air Staff, Sir Charles Portal. 'I'll have a word with him,' said Mary, 'about being more punctual in future.'

Time passed at Sandtoft, and no posting came for me to Lancasters or Mosquitoes, or any other sort of aircraft. Nothing but the clumsy Halifax. The re-formation of the crew had been a dream that vanished in the harsh reality of

Air Force life. Lanham was homeward-bound for Perth, Myring for a little town near Melbourne; Walker had gone from Blyton to join the PFF; Fairbairn was on special duties with a Liberator squadron; Protheroe was studying point-five Brownings and the Boulton-Paul turret at an aerodrome near York, with a view to being the belly-gunner of a Halifax Mark III. All I could do was make a nuisance of myself with anyone who had to do with postings and, meanwhile, trundle round the skies of Lincolnshire, send my pupils on their way to squadrons, and vent my spleen on opening batsmen whenever Crummy handed me the ball.

A great Mess party was ordained, the first of its kind that I had seen. Served by half-a-dozen stewards in white jackets, a temporary trestled bar stretched all the way down one wall of the anteroom while, in the games room, linen-covered ping-pong tables bore a spread that would have made Lord Woolton suck his teeth and for which, that we might not fail to do it justice, Johnson and I had fasted for two days. Everyone looked peculiarly smart in unaccustomed 'best blue' uniforms, with buttons shined and trousers pressed by dedicated batwomen; local dignitaries attended, pink-cheeked and stiff in evening dress; chums came from other airfields in the Group: Cassidy, Cameron and Knight from Blyton, Rory and his friend from Wickenby, people from Ludford, Binbrook, Elsham Wolds and Bawtry. Perspiring freely, the steelworks band played foxtrots, quicksteps, waltzes, tangoes and, as the night wore on, even the occasional, somewhat heavy-footed rumba.

Watching the orchestra with massive calm, Watson gave a sudden chuckle. 'They remind me of the one about the Accrington Stanley Glassworks Brass Band,' he said, 'Have you heard it?'

We had not, but that was a situation he would rectify. 'Well, they were giving an open-air concert, were this band, and blokes were going round houses in the neighbourhood with collecting boxes. This particular bloke knocks and rings and bangs for ages on one door, and at last some old codger opens it just a crack and says "What d'yer want?"

"Making a collection, sir, for the Accrington Stanley Glassworks Brass Band," says the bloke and rattles his box. "Eh?"

The bloke tells him again, a bit louder. "You'll 'ave ter speak up, young feller," says the old codger, "I'm 'ard of 'earing."

"The Accrington Stanley Glassworks Brass Band," shouts the bloke in the old chap's ear. "I'm collecting for them."

"You what?"

The bloke gives it up, see, and he's just walking off down the pavement when the old codger calls out after him. " 'Ere, shut the gate, shall yer, young feller."

So the bloke goes back and shuts it, muttering to himself "bugger the gate", and the old chap cackles "aye, and bugger the Accrington Stanley Glassworks Brass Band an' all".'

The whole occasion, including food, drinks, band and Watson's jokes, cost ten bob apiece on Mess bills. To say my conscience hurt me would be false – there had to be some recompense for flying the Halifax and sweating under Crummy's yoke – but I could not help contrasting the quantity and quality of food with what my mother's rations, for example, were. For each of them at home, she could buy 31 eggs a year and, by the week, one shilling and twopence worth of meat, two ounces each of butter, fat, cheese and tea, eight of sugar, four of jam and bacon, three of sweets. These were the items 'on the ration', for which she gave up coupons in the shop. 'Personal points' were also in the book, and she could use these as she chose for such commodities, if and when available, as canned fruit, condensed milk, 'spam', rice, biscuits, cereals and baked beans. Potatoes, bread and most varieties of vegetable were never rationed, but the 'National Loaf', made perforce from British wheat that in peacetime would be fed to cattle, found little favour with the public, who categorised it as dirty, dark and indigestible. The consumption of potatoes as a filler, therefore, was massively encouraged in the press and on the hoardings by 'Potato Pete', a cartoon character as plumply, lumpily genial as the Minister of Food appeared to be himself, and 'Doctor Carrot' exhorted Britain to turn to him as substitute for fruit. Strangely enough, so Lord Woolton's people said, more milk was being drunk that year than in the year before the war.

But more malt than milk was being consumed at Sandtoft's famous party, and I had my share. Woody and Eric Nelson had appeared, coming late from Blyton, and their queries about 'young Gracie' prompted me to ring her there and then. The revels now were reaching a crescendo, and I had the feeling that my small jokes and casual endearments lost a little of their impact when they had to be repeated, forte, several times.

'I'm awfully sorry you're not here,' I bawled, 'but you needn't worry, I'm getting along fine with the Mayor of Doncaster's daughter.'

'I can't hear a word. Have you ever thought of ringing me when you're not at a pub or a party?'

'Of course I have. But I spend most of my time in an aeroplane, and I can't seem to get you on Channel 9.'

This was not entirely true, but there was some basis for the observation: of seven flying instructors in B Flight, two were posted, two on courses, one (and who could blame him?) had gone sick. Nevertheless, I had the promise of three days off in August, Nina had contrived the same, and two rooms were reserved at an hotel on the Great North Road, past the race-track south of Doncaster. 'Are you still all right for Punch's,' I shouted, 'or shall I ask the Mayor's daughter instead?'

'I can't hear you, Jack. Is your leave still on?'

I gave it up, and joined in with the band. 'Dreams enfold you; in them, dear, I'll hold you; so I'll say good night, sweetheart, goodnight.'

As I put the 'phone down, a passing Flight Lieutenant eyed me narrowly. I recognised him as one of the P Staff officers at Group Headquarters, whom I had pestered for a posting many times. He shied away nervously as I lurched towards him, but turned back as a thought appeared to cross his mind. 'Listen, old boy,' he said, glancing this way and that along the corridor, in the confidential way that junior staff officers tended to adopt, 'you're always binding about getting back on ops. Something came through this morning that might be just the job.'

'Jolly good. Come and have a drink, and tell me all about it. I've always known they couldn't win the war without me.'

It was quite easy to catch the barman's attention. All you had to do was break a glass. 'Cheers,' I said. 'Now, what does Mr Churchill want me to do?'

'It's four engines.'

'Yes?'

'It's operational.'

'Go on.'

'It's towing gliders.'

I took a long, slow drink of beer. 'Towing them where?'

'I don't know, old boy. Across the jolly old Rhine, I suppose. I mean, we've got to cross it sometime, haven't we?'

I caught the barman's attention again. 'There's no need to do that, sir,' he said, 'I'd have come when I saw you was empty.'

'It's not beer I want, Cecil – well, I will have another, since you mention it – it was really your advice.'

'Advice, sir?'

'They want me to tow gliders full of soldiers into Germany, Cecil. What do you reckon – should I do it?'

Cecil shook his head. 'You know what they say, sir – never volunteer for nothing.'

'Okay, Settle, that Cecils it. I'll give it a go.'

The Staff Officer said that he would put my name up for the job.

'Wait a minute,' I said, 'what if a posting comes through for Mossies, or for going back on Lancs?'

'Don't worry about that – whichever comes through first, you'll get.' He took a swig of beer and wiped a little froth from his moustache. 'What's the matter with you, anyway, old boy? Are you some sort of gong-hunter?' He pointed at the ribbons on my chest. 'Aren't you satisfied with those?'

'It's nothing to do with the gongs: they don't mean a thing. Well, sometimes they do, but it isn't that.' The thoughts churned in my head, too thick, too quick, for me to give them words. Pride, and self-esteem, the bugle's call, the lust for danger, the need to go on fighting fear, the company of the characters – cynical and stoic – who flew on operations, the sense of loss at not being of their number.

'It's Cecil's doing. I always take his advice on the important things – how many pints to have, when to go in for dinner, when to go to bed. And when to go back on ops.'

The barman faced me squarely, both hands on the bar. 'Don't you go putting the blame on me, sir. I said never volunteer for nothing.'

I stared into his eyes. He had a narrow, long-nosed face, with a good-humoured mouth and laugh-lines on his cheeks. I quite liked Cecil's face. The Staff Officer's face was not so likeable, when I looked at it closely. The moustache was reminiscent of an armpit, and the eyebrows met above a red-veined nose. I began to examine other faces in the room, and did not care for any of them. Eyes were small and hard, or wide and vacant; mouths were rigid or loose-lipped; ears, on the whole, looked quite ridiculous. Suddenly I realised what was wrong. All of these faces belonged to men, and none of them to women. There was a serious lack of women in that room. I emptied my glass – which Cecil promptly took out of my hand – and made off in the general direction of the music.

There were plenty of women on the dance floor, but they were all with other fellows. I moved among them for a while then, failing to find a spare one, took up a strategic position by the wall and waited for somebody to happen. The piece of wall I chose to lean against turned out to be a service-door into the kitchen, and I thought it spoke a lot for the standard of physical agility we ace pilots could maintain that I was able to run backwards for fully fifteen paces before collapsing on the floor. A stifled shriek drew my attention to a blonde batwoman who, having been engaged in pushing out the buffet sweetmeats earlier in the evening, was seated at a kitchen table scoffing the remains. 'Hello, Jean,' I said, 'You're just the girl I wanted to see. Come and have a dance.'

'Eh?'

'Dancing, Jean, to music. You know, me going forwards, you going backwards. They're playing 'Cheek to Cheek'.'

She laughed, brushing a flake of puff-pastry off her shirt. 'Come off it, sir. I'm not allowed in there, as well you know.'

I stood up. 'Yes, you are – special dispensation for tonight. We've been fighting for democracy for five years, and we've finally decided to give it a go at Sandtoft. Come on, Jean, let's have you!'

Everything was fine until somebody turned a spotlight on. I did not like being spotlighted. Sober, it made me fidgety: unsober, it brought on the flee-or-fight reaction. In London, once, I had knocked the torch from a policeman's hand when he shone it in my face, and that had taken some explaining. Now, I grabbed the girl and ran. The spotlight followed, and I took evasive action. A grinning officer stood in the way, moving as I moved. I seized a handful of his shirt-front, pulled him off his balance, and pushed with all my strength. With a crash of breaking glass and woodwork, he reeled across a table, and the spotlight showed a last glimpse of the shock upon his face as the swing-doors shut behind us.

'Told you I shouldn't have been in there,' said Jean, shaking the illicit page-boy bob upon her shoulders. 'You got the wind up, didn't you? I thought you would, once you sobered up a bit. You've had a couple, haven't you, sir?'

'I didn't get the wind up. Not about you anyway. I just

wanted to get out of there.'

'Did you, sir? Well, I'd never have guessed.' She gave a squeal of laughter. 'Poor Flying Officer Jukes – no, honest, you shouldn't have chucked him about like that.'

'He shouldn't have got in the way.' I looked into the smiling blue eyes. 'No, you're right, Jean. I'll go and say I'm sorry.'

'No, not now, sir. Least said, soonest mended. You'll both have forgotten all about it by morning.' She led me to the bench on which I first had found her. 'Sit down there, and I'll make a cup of coffee. Then you're going to bed.'

I glared at her retreating back, and the rounded buttocks, wagging impertinently beneath the grey-blue skirt. The cheek of the girl! An Aircraftwoman – well, all right, a Leading Aircraftwoman – telling an acting Flight Lieutenant what to do. Ordering him about! But then, girls were like that, if you gave them half a chance. I lowered myself onto the bench, leaned back against the wall, and loosened my collar. After that, things went out of focus. I had an occasional impression of very laboured movement, the cool air of the night upon my face, and the sound of girlish giggles; but the first thing I knew clearly was the face of Norma in the morning light, standing over me with a mug of tea in hand, while I lay, pyjama-clad, in bed. 'Where's Jean, indeed,' she snorted. 'That's a fine question to ask, that is. She was up half the night, as you know well enough, sir, and she's getting some kip.'

I tried to consider all the implications of the girl's remarks, but the effort made my head ache. 'Why didn't you let me get some kip, then? Instead of waking me up with your beastly tea.'

'Because you're OC Day, that's why, sir, and flying begins in half-an-hour. I'll take the tea away then, shall I?'

'No, I'll drink it, just to please you, if it kills me.' It was real batwoman's tea, dark and sweet, with specks of powdered milk and tea-leaves floating on the surface. Norma took my best blue from the wardrobe and my shoes from underneath the bed. 'I say, Norma...'

'It's no good asking me to bring you breakfast – I haven't got time. You can get it in the Mess if you hurry.'

'It's not that – I don't feel like breakfast, anyway. Did Jean put me to bed last night?'

'Don't you remember?'

'I wouldn't ask you if I did, would I?'

She stood in the doorway, looking at me over her shoulder. 'We both did, if you must know.' There was a sudden flash of small, white teeth. 'You're not near as heavy as my dad.'

While I fooled about like this at Sandtoft, the war was taking a more serious turn for people in the south-east of the country, as the enemy's dwindling offensive capability took on a new dimension, and the V2 rocket succeeded the V1. Unlike the doodle-bug, which announced its coming with the eructating racket and the sudden silence of its engine, the V2 fell out of the stratosphere without a warning – a twelve-ton missile with a ton of high-explosive in its nose. Early in the evening of 8th September, the first killed three, and maimed another ten, of Chiswick's population; thereafter, two or three fell every day until 17th, when Allied airborne soldiers crossed the Lower Rhine at Arnhem, and caused the German High Command to move their rocket-launchers further east.

A 5 Group mission on the night of 11th despatched 200 Lancasters to Darmstadt, while 50 Mosquitoes bombed Berlin as a diversion, and 70 aircraft of 100 Group interfered with electronics and strafed the fighter bases. The death of some 10,000 Germans put the V2 in a sort of grim perspective. Nevertheless, the rocket, unpredictable of impact, impossible of interception, soon returned and was bad news for the civil population at a moment when they had begun to hope the tide had turned.

But, for the men who flew the bombers, the war was getting much less disagreeable. As the soldiers fought their way through France, they deprived the Fatherland of the early warning system on which the night fighters depended. Furthermore, the bombers' radar aids, the Oboe and G-H transmitters, moving east behind the soldiers, increased the killing range. 'Do you know,' asked Johnson, 'what I reckon? It's a bleeding sight safer on ops now than flying these ropey bleeding Halibags.'

'Are you going to put in for a second tour, then Mugsey?'

'Who, me?' He did his gulping act. 'Not me, Butch. I'm not all that keen to shift from here, tell you the truth. Know what I mean?'

I knew what he meant. The landlord's daughter had the Londoner in thrall. That was another of the troubles about girls: unless you were a man of iron, they tended to make the native hue of resolution turn a little pale – as Hamlet mentioned in another context. If you showed me a fellow who was potty about some girl, I would be fairly sure of showing you a fellow who, if he did not actually shrink from juggling with Jesus, was unlikely to be first man in the queue. Samson's experience with Delilah was a case in point. If you really got down to serious thinking about the influence of girls, 'insidious' could well be the word which sprang into your mind. And no one was invulnerable. Luckily, I had the advantage over Johnson – over Hamlet too, and Samson, if it came to that – of being born in Sheffield, which was known to put a little steel into the soul. It was true that, under the influence of alcohol and Tiny Watson, I had mentioned to Nina Gracie that I loved her, and there would be those who discerned an element of pottiness in that. They would be mistaken. We Sheffielders are not that sort of people.

Yet, now I came to think about it, my father – than whom none was more of a Sheffielder – had always seemed slightly potty about my mother. Perhaps he was the exception that proved the rule – he was, in many ways, an exceptional kind of man. Nevertheless, the watchword must be vigilance for, just as flying did not mix with grog (vide

Lanham, 1943 et seq), no more did Jesus-juggling mix with pottiness about girls.

Having undertaken this appraisal, and been convinced by all the evidence, it was particularly shocking to hear my own voice, breathless with emotion, in the empty midnight blackness of the Punch's forecourt, uttering the well-known, rhetorical enquiry. Nelson probably had a similar sensation when he told the surgeon to get busy on his arm, and Charles the First, yet more so, when he gave the executioner the nod. I supposed that in their situations, as in mine at Punch's, there just seemed to be nothing else for them to say.

Until then, I had been as happy as a sandboy. She had burst into that honest laughter at my jokes, joined in all my Crosby songs (she was jolly good at harmony), told me the news of London and listened to what was fit to tell of Sandtoft. Cuddling had broken out, and kissing. Yielding lips, cool cheeks, soft hair, the tightening embrace that promised passion – and at last the night, the witching hour, the need, had brought me to that state and statement of surrender. The matter settled, we kissed again, with a solemnity befitting the occasion, and I climbed weak-kneed, heavy with destiny, dizzy with wonder, up the Punch's staircase to my bed.

When I walked into the 'B' Flight office two days later, the Flight Commander raised his eyebrows. 'Bless my soul, I'd almost forgotten you were on the strength. Decent of you to look in, old boy.'

That was what I liked about Ken Major – his tremendous sense of humour. I tipped somebody's parachute out of a chair. 'It's nice to be missed,' I said. 'Gives you a sort of warm glow inside. I've been on a forty-eight, if you must know.'

He examined a calendar on the wall – the one that showed the Daily Mirror's Jane in her usual state. 'Forty-eight?'

'Well, it may have stretched an hour or two at both ends. You wouldn't begrudge me that, would you, with all the overtime I do?'

'No such thing as overtime in the Service, old boy. An officer is on duty 24 hours a day, seven days a week. Anyway, you're posted.'

If my heart did not actually miss a beat, it certainly took a two-bar rest. 'Where to?'

'Siberia, on a snow-clearance course.'

The idle pilots in the office giggled. He really did have a marvellous sense of fun.

'Right,' I said, 'I'll go pack, and draw a shovel out of stores.'

'Some place called Bridgnorth, actually, Jack. Can't say I've ever heard of it. A 'P' Staff chap at Group rang through – something to do with gliders.'

I discovered from the Adjutant that the course at Bridgnorth – wherever it might be – was to assemble on 1st November. Three weeks' annual leave were due to me, and I determined to take two before I went. The feast to Bacchus that ensued at Sandtoft marked, not merely my departure, but the first fogs of October, which kept the aircraft on the ground and my mess-mates in the bar. It was as well that Cecil's attitude to overtime was much the same as Major's, for the party lasted a liquid thirty-six hours.

My last flight in the Halifax – before the orgy started – had been unusually enjoyable. Maybe a sixth sense told me, despite what the P Staff man had said, that time and many trials would pass before I held four throttle-levers in my palm again; maybe it was the patchwork quilt of gold and green and brown beneath, the silky white drift of cloud beside me and the cold, pale blue above; whatever the reason, it was a magic hour, with the mighty aircraft steady and obedient in my hands. I did not want to land.

Bleary-eyed on the train to London, squatting on my cases in the corridor, I reviewed the money situation for a while and found it far from sound. The three days at Punch's had not been all that expensive (bed and breakfast, with early morning tea, £1 16s 8d, dinner ten shillings), and Nina, claiming that her monthly pay was within a few pounds of mine, had insisted that she pay her way; furthermore, I had lived with the frugality of a Tibetan monk for the remainder of September, during which a nett income of £29 9s 3d against expenditure of £22 6s 2d showed a saving that might have satisfied Mr Micawber's criterion for happiness, but only served to cut my overdraft from twenty-four to eighteen pounds. I concluded that the Tibetan habit would have to be maintained, not only through my leave, but far into a future I had so recently come to think of as foreseeable.

That conclusion took a knock when, on my first day home, a telegram arrived, from the Adjutant. 'Leave to be regarded as embarkation leave stop,' it read. 'Further instructions will follow by post.'

Again, my thoughts ran back to Beryl: I had evaded a commitment to that curly-headed charmer on the grounds that people ought to leave their options open when one of them was posted overseas. To be consistent, I should say the same to Nina now. But inconsistency was not a sin, merely a tickle of the conscience, a realisation that expediency, selfishness and maybe plain old love, were impulses that worked, for good or ill.

The vicar of St Mary's Church, on Harrow Hill, was the Reverend Woolley, unusual among Ministers of God in that he had a World War One VC. Ashen-faced and gaunt, he propped himself up in the bed to which an ailment had confined him and addressed us sternly. 'Unfortunately I shall be unable to perform the ceremony myself, as I am not so well as I would wish to be at the moment. Mr Carpenter, my curate, will undertake the duty. I understand the arrangements are in hand, despite the very short notice you have given us. Now, I am going to ask you one or two questions...'

He put us through a formidable grilling as to the condition of our hearts and minds. Reflecting on the matter later, I guessed it was his illness that made him seem so forbidding, so uncongenial a minister. I was uncomfortable in his presence, and masked a feeling of hostility with an unnatural heartiness, but Nina was cool and sensible, pleasant and polite. When he briefly called on God to make us good, she knelt, I bowed my head and then, released, ran halfway down the hill, leaping and turning in the air, whooping and throwing my arms about while she, alternately laughing and admonishing, half-trotting, half-briskly walking, followed on behind.

'The bride,' reported the *Harrow Observer*, under a photograph from which it seemed that Nina was bravely doing her best to hold me upright, 'was given away by her father. She wore uniform. The Rev. E. F. Carpenter officiated, and the best man was Flying Officer J. Cassidy, DFC, RAAF. The service was choral, with Mr Arnold Grier at the organ. The choir included boys from the Lower School of John Lyon, where the bridegroom was formerly a pupil. Owing to Service exigencies the wedding was held at very short notice.'

It was the head, O. A. Le Beau himself, who, in prompt answer to my mother's call, had provided choristers and summoned the great organist from London. It was he, in theologian's black, with corded, golden pince-nez on his nose and silver wings of hair – always a little longer than the fashion – about his ears, who strolled with me among the tombstones, chatting soothingly, while Mr Harris's total fleet of taxis swept up to the ancient lychgate, disgorging parents, hastily-transported relatives, half the female complement of Whitmore Road and its environs, an anxious Cassidy and a trio of gorgeous Whitehall WAAFs who were to be the bridesmaids.

'Getting married tomorrow,' I had cabled Sandtoft, 'request seven days extension on passionate grounds.'

When the rites were over, and the saturnine head waiter (another friend of old) hovered at my elbow with a constant fountain of champagne, Cassidy stood front and centre in the King's Head reception room, reading out the telegrams. 'This one's from Sandtoft,' he said, and glanced at me. 'I don't know whether...'

'Go ahead, Jim. What's the message?'

'Okay. It says "Congratulations on your marriage, stop. You've had your time, stop. Imperative report Bridgnorth 1st November." Aw, gee, Jack, wouldn't it rock yer? Still, never mind, you've got five days.'

'And nights,' suggested a cheerful uncle, in a rasping whisper. The company murmured sympathetically, Nina squeezed my arm, and the waiter put more bubbles in my glass.

Any hope we might have had of anonymity, at the old inn by the riverside at Marlow, were quickly dashed by Mary's waiting telegram ('Welcome to Compleat Angler—Bang on—Press on regardless—Whizzo—Much love'), and by the flowers and wine placed on our table with the compliments of the management. Proud of my bride, momentarily secure, and warm with happiness, I responded gladly to the kindly smiles and nods of other diners, while Nina dimpled, blushed and kept her eyes demurely on her soup. Five days and nights passed like an autumn leaf blown in the wind. Full board and residence for the two of us cost £15 18s 6d, and the Westminster Bank at Harrow ordered more red ink.

5

Combat Course

The only other occupant of the cheerless anteroom at Bridgnorth was a sturdy Flight Lieutenant, unusually advanced in years for one of that rank, whose face I felt I knew. I sat down with my glass of beer, not so near as to intrude but not so far away as to seem deliberately unsociable. After a few minutes, he fractionally lowered a copy of *The Times* and looked at me above his spectacles. 'Evenin',' he grunted.

'Good evening.'

'Only time of day a fellow gets a chance to read the paper in peace.'

'I shan't disturb you.'

'New here, aren't you?'

I admitted I had arrived within the hour.

Steady, blue eyes studied me, while I tried to remember where I had seen that face before. His shoulders bore the flashes of the RAF Regiment, his breast a row of ribbons, few of which I recognised. 'Operational type, eh,' he observed. 'What were you on?'

'Lancs.'

'Care for the other half?'

When he had fetched the drinks and lowered himself into his seat, he embarked upon a careful tobacco-pouch and pipe routine. 'My name's Bruce,' he said.

The name clicked with the features. I saw the stalwart figure plodding through Hollywood's notion of a London fog, while Basil Rathbone whispered, 'You have your Service revolver in your pocket, Watson?'

'I thought your face was familiar,' I said. 'How's the Hound of the Baskervilles?'

'Who? Oh, I see. You take me for my kid brother, Nigel, the cinema actor. I'm Michael – Sir Michael, as a matter of fact, but I'd rather you called me Mike.'

I introduced myself, and he asked what brought me to the wilds of Shropshire. When I told him, he took the pipe out of his mouth and shook his head. 'You won't find any gliders to tug at Bridgnorth.'

'Oh? What happens here, then?'

Between sips of whisky and extensive servicing operations on his pipe, he revealed that what happened there was a combat course for glider pilots. Hitherto, it seemed, when somebody had been required to fly a glider into action, a likely soldier had been taught the rudiments of flight and put into the cockpit. This expedient, in operations, had not proved wholly satisfactory, and it had therefore been decided to try another option. There were newly-qualified young pilots everywhere you looked. The Commonwealth Training Scheme had yielded an abundance – so many that the Squadrons could not use them all. Even the gaping maw of Bomber Command was overflowing. Why not, some lateral thinker on the Staff had cried, teach these fledglings how to fight? That way, more gliders might attain their targets in one piece, more airborne troops their battlegrounds.

Yes, I thought, as I listened to the reasoning, and if these pilots, once their flying task was over and their passengers in action, proved not to have entirely mastered all the military arts, it could not matter less. There would be plenty more where they came from. But where did I – the driver, airframes, multi-engined – fit into this piece of rationalising? It was no concern of mine who flew the glider, or what training he had undergone. My task, once I had towed him to the target and wished him happy landings, was complete. I decided to probe a little deeper and, for a start, to find out more of my informant.

'Me, old boy? I'm by way of being your Senior Weapons Instructor. Bren, Sten, rifle, pistol, all that sort of thing. Everything bar grenades and mortars. Can't ever seem to think of them as suitable weapons for an officer, can you? 'Fortunately, there's a Brown job who has to do with them. Bit of a roughneck, if you ask me, but quite a sound chap in his way.'

He broke off to do something to his pipe-stem. When he had reassembled the device, he chuckled fruitily. 'Suppose I'm a bit of a roughneck myself, if it comes to that. Fought in every scrap since the Boer War, all over the world. Always been a fighting family, y'know, ever since our founder, Robert the Bruce himself.'

I took a sip of beer and looked at him thoughtfully for a moment. 'You mentioned being my Weapons Instructor…'

'Senior Weapons Instructor, old boy. I have a few NCOs and lads to give me a hand.'

'Yes, I'm sure you do, but I think there must be some mistake. I don't really need to know much about weapons. You see, I'm not here to fly the gliders - I'm here to tow them.'

He frowned, with the match poised above the pipe-bowl. 'You'll have a job, old boy. As I say there aren't any gliders here, let alone tugs. Just the combat course.'

The next two weeks gave ample proof that he was absolutely right. Everywhere you looked at Bridgnorth there were rifle-ranges, pistol-targets, parapets from which you threw grenades, ditches in which you lay and waited for something horrible to happen. You could never go from one place to another at that station without climbing over, crawling under, or fighting your way through, some unpleasant obstacle. Explosions, detonations, nasty smells and sudden flashes were everyday (and every night) accompaniments of life. Even sitting in a classroom, listening to a nice, quiet lecture on such a simple operation as choking somebody to death with a piece of knotted string, you could be sure that a couple of thunderflashes would be tossed in through the window to enliven the experience.

Most of the victims of this calculated violence were the

fledgling pilots, eager, fresh-faced lads, whose need for action had made them volunteer for flying without engines when they realised that, the way the war was going, there would be no other path to glory for them to pursue. Gittins and Archbold, however, were ex-bomber men like me, and it soon became apparent why we were there. Our future duty, it transpired, would be to act as Flight Commanders, to lead the lads in battle when the gliders landed, and every pilot had to earn his keep.

A tepid shower-bath had removed some of the evidence of an afternoon's acquaintance with a noisome drainage-pipe, when I put the point to Gittins. 'Did you volunteer for this?'

He paused in the act of towelling his thinning hair and glared at me. 'I may look a bit bloody simple,' he snarled, 'but I'm not stark, raving mad. Why, did you?'

I shook my head. 'They told me they wanted heavy-bomber chaps to fly the tugs.'

'Yeah, that's what the crafty sods told me.'

'And me,' said Archbold, wincing as he squeezed sore feet into the unaccustomed boots.

I buckled webbing gaiters round the trouser-bottoms of my new khaki battledress. 'The sprogs are all volunteers,' I said. 'I mean, real volunteers – not just you, you and you. They had the choice of flying as flight-engineers, ground duties or this.'

'Yes, well, that's their horrible luck, isn't it,' said Gittins. 'But I've gone grey in the service of Bomber Command, and I don't reckon to finish the war with a bayonet up my arse.'

Arnold gave a hollow laugh. 'You know what they say – if you can't take a joke you shouldn't have joined.'

Next day, Sir Michael's minions sent me for a quiet walk with a Sten gun. 'Keep your eyes peeled, Sir,' said the sergeant, 'there's Jerry soldiers in them woods. Some of ours, an' all. You can tell the difference between a Jerry uniform an' ours, can you, Sir?'

'I'm not sure, sergeant,' I admitted. 'Perhaps some instinct will tell me which is which.'

He regarded me with eyes. like stone. 'Let's hope so, Sir. Because what you've got to do is shoot the Jerries, all right, Sir? Shoot them buggers dead, and not shoot ours.'

I fingered the Sten gun's magazine. 'These rounds are live, you know, sergeant.'

'Perfectly correct, Sir. But the soldiers aren't – they're made of cardboard.' He gave the briefest of chuckles, as though he had very few chuckles left and did not want to waste them. 'The success of the whole mission might depend on this patrol, all right, Sir? And it—is—starting—NOW!'

I followed the painted arrows through the wood on tiptoe, holding the gun across my chest and letting the eyeballs, long cultivated at Lieutenant Sena's will, rove in all directions. There, on the right, among the bushes, a scowling, grey-clad figure crouched. I threw the iron butt-plate to my shoulder, aimed the barrel at the figure's chest and, with no more than a momentary batting of the eyelids, squeezed the trigger. Little happened: the dummy's scowl seemed to become a sneer, the painted rifle was still pointed at my vital parts. Unhesitatingly, I released the safety catch and tried again. This time, the clatter of the Sten rang through the wood, and I saw the figure jerk, before the rim of my steel helmet, jolting forward, hid it from my sight. It was the work of a moment to thrust the helmet back, and to observe that my antagonist was flat upon the ground. I pulled the chin-strap tighter and remorselessly continued the patrol.

Ten minutes later (or it might have been an hour, for time was difficult to tell), I confronted the final target. This one was depicted in the position of surrender, and that was just as well, as I had expended all three magazines of Sten gun ammunition, and been obliged to fall back on the Webley pistol, with which I was by no means sure to hit the nearest, largest tree.

Sir Michael stolled out of the copse behind me. 'Not bad,' he grunted. 'Six of theirs, and only three of ours. Like the Sten do you?'

'It's a super weapon,' I admitted, 'but, look here, Mike, my weapon is a bomber. I shouldn't really be here.'

He regarded me thoughtfully, slapping the side of his leg with the cane he liked to carry. 'I'm poppin' up to town for the weekend,' he revealed. 'Care to come along? I've got a thing at the Air House on Saturday, but we could take a snort or two on Friday evenin' somewhere, and travel back together on Sunday.'

'Somewhere' turned out to be the cocktail bar at the Savoy, where my steps had never previously led. Piccadilly Hotel, yes; Strand Palace, Regent Palace, certainly; but never to that little passage off the Strand. The 'snorts' were ordered by Sir Michael. 'Large Scotch, Eddy, a light ale and one for yourself. Oh, and Eddy, put it on the slate, would you?'

I regarded the man with a new, and deep, respect. To order drinks on tick was rare in Middlesex; in Lincolnshire and Yorkshire, practically unknown. In the deepest heart of London I had thought it inconceivable, and yet clearly Mike possessed the knack, for the barman – immaculate in bow tie and monkey-jacket – smirked respectfully and, with a flourish, did as he was bade.

Having supervised the imperceptible dilution of his Scotch with soda-water, my hero cast a lowering glance around the room. 'Bit early for anybody to be in yet,' he observed, thus carelessly consigning the dozen or so impeccably-dressed, politely-chatting patrons to the category of non-persons. 'Let's sit down and have a pow-wow.' We collected stools and settled at the bar. 'Shouldn't talk shop, of course, he mumbled, 'but I've been mullin' over what you said. I mean, about a mistake over your postin'. You see, I don't think there has been any mistake.'

I tore my attention away from the splendid, softly-lighted decor of the place, and the stylised frenzy of the cocktail-shaking Eddy. 'Don't you, Mike?'

'No, old boy. I think you were railroaded, but for a damn good reason.'

'Really? I'm blowed if I can think of one.'

'The lads need you, old boy.'

'What lads?'

'The sprog pilots,' he explained, pronouncing the word as 'peel-ohs'. 'They respect you, you see, being an operational type and all that. They'll follow you, silly young buggers – that's important in a scrap.'

'I don't want them to follow me. I don't want anything to do with them. Look, Mike, I didn't mind losing my second ring to go back on heavies, or Mossies. But not to fly a wooden packing-case and play at soldiers.'

He chuckled tolerantly. 'Nonsense. I've had my eye on you. You're enjoyin' every minute of it, and you'll make a jolly good Flight Commander.'

'Enjoying it!' I spluttered, 'I've got filthy dirty every day, been half-deafened most of the time, nearly lost my finger in a Bren gun, had two teeth out, practically without anaesthetic, by that maniac of a dentist, and I'll tell you another thing – I hate this fizzy bottled beer.'

'Why didn't you say so?' He beckoned to the barman. 'Eddy'll find you a pint of cooking ale somewhere.'

Eddy's assistant was dispatched ('since it's for a friend of yours, Sir Michael'), and I imagined him tiptoeing across the Strand, silver-plated jug in hand, to the nearest four-ale bar. Mike reverted to his theme. 'Reminds me of somethin' I said to Winnie, about a year ago,' he rumbled.

'Winnie?'

'Winston, old boy, Prime Minister. Known him for years, of course.'

'Of course.'

'He was gettin' off an aeroplane at Northolt, comin' back from some conference, you know. I happened to be on the fringe of the crowd that was there to meet him. Well, I've never been a fellow to push himself forward. But dash it, he spotted me right away. Beckoned me over, though all the brass hats…' He guffawed at the memory, and tapped his glass on the bar. 'Same again, Eddy, and where's that damn beer?'

'Coming right up, Sir Michael.'

'Fellow's dyin' of thirst here. Anyway, as I was tellin' you. "Hello, Mike," says Winnie in that growly way of his, "and how the devil are you?" I was in RAF uniform, you know, and I threw him up a salute. "The RAF's doin' jolly well," says he, "winnin' the war for us." And I made bold enough to tell him what I thought. "Bombers are all very well, sir," I said, "but we shan't beat the Hun until our chaps are marchin' on German soil."

A foaming pewter tankard appeared at my elbow, and I drank his health.

'Cheers, old boy,' he said. 'Anyway, that's all I wanted to mention. You probably think I'm a silly old buffer, but I know a bit about warfare – all I bally well do know, actually.' His pale, blue eyes swept round the bar, and fell upon a group of Free French sailors, who had entered while he talked. With them were some notably well-favoured women, and it was to the most spectacular of these, a girl with shoulder-length, almost white blonde hair and a vivid, laughing face, that he addressed himself. 'Fanny, my dear,' he cried, 'how marvellous to see you! Leave those dreadful matelots at once, and come amongst me.'

He planted a soldierly salute upon the lady's creamy cheek, and introduced her as Frances Day, the well-known entertainer. Me, he introduced as the unknown bomber pilot. Struggling to survive in this rarefied society, I offered the opinion that her recording of 'Long Ago and Far Away' was absolutely super. She gave me the well-known delta-shaped smile and the well-known up-from-under look. 'How sweet of you to say so, darling. But Dorothy Carless made that one.'

'Of course. I meant "That Lovely Weekend"'

'Vera Lynn, darling. But you're getting warmer.'

She was so right: warmer and stickier. To the rescue came the good Sir Michael, crooning, in a husky baritone: 'It's delightful, it's delicious, it's dee-lovely!'

Laying aside her cocktail glass, the lady whispered the refrain.

'The night is fine,

The moon is clear,

And if you want to go walking, dear…'

We all joined in the chorus: Mike and I, the girls, several other drinkers, even Eddy and assistant. 'C'est bien,' called a sailor, 'bravo!'

'I understand

The reason why

You're sentimental, 'cause so am I,' sang the well-known entertainer.

'It's delightful,' roared the chorus, 'it's delicious, it's dee-lovely!'

'Encore, encore!' the sailors cried. Singing broke out in all directions: down the Strand and into Mooney's Irish Drinking House, in taxis and in unknown, dimly-lighted bars. It was later, disgracefully much later, that the call to Harrow, sanity and duty, filtered through. Somehow I was at Baker Street, feeling in my raincoat pocket for the railway ticket and finding something warm and soft and hairy there. I pulled it out and showed it to the ticket-collector. 'It's a puppy,' I muttered, 'How the devil did that get there?'

'Couldn't say, I'm sure, sir.'

'I think it's eaten my ticket.'

'Oh, dear.'

'Yes, it has. Look, there's a little bit of it left.'

'Never mind, sir, you can easily get another one. The ticket-office is just over there.'

'You wouldn't accept this bit as a ticket?'

He did not even bother to shake his head: he simply looked at me with his ticket-collector eyes. The animal was trying to eat my thumb as a dessert.

'You could clip the puppy's ear,' I suggested. 'I mean, the rest of the ticket's inside it.'

'Would you mind standing aside, sir? Gentleman's trying to get through.'

I could not bring myself to leave the puppy on the train, nor on the slowly-moving, late-night bus that took me to the end of Whitmore Road. I thought of dropping it across the fence into the Philathletic Ground – the 'Phil' – which lay on one side of the road or, and this was an attractive notion, into a kindly neighbour's garden. There could be no doubt that the Peplers, Reals or Bannisters, even the Andersons, would give it a good home. But the creature was still there, in my pocket, when my dressing-gowned father took my hand at the door of No 88.

In the morning, over the fried spam and potatoes, I was berated by my mother and by Nina (who, for the weekend, had left her room on Harrow Hill in preference for mine), while the puppy made small secret puddles on the kitchen floor. 'I can't imagine what you were thinking of,' my mother said, 'letting somebody give you a puppy…'

'I didn't actually know they were giving it to me, Mummy, I told you – I found it in my pocket.'

'Nonsense, dear. People don't just find puppies in their pockets. And what are you going to do with it?'

'I thought I might take it up in a glider and throw it out.'

My father paused in the act of scraping a film of margarine across his toast. 'Oh, I don't think that would be the thing to do, old fellow…'

Fond as he was of his little joke, his perception of other people's was sometimes less than supersonic.

'All right, Daddy. If you rather I didn't…'

'Nina can't possibly have it in her digs,' pursued my mother.

'No,' agreed my wife, 'and I don't think my Air Commodore would be awfully pleased if it did in the War Room what it's doing now.'

The animal was banished to the garden, and some mopping-up ensued. 'What are you going to call it, anyway?' asked Nina.

'I wasn't thinking of calling it anything. I don't really want to get to know it all that well.'

She gave the laugh, half-shocked, half-tickled, that I had come to hope for. 'We'll have to call it something.'

'All right. We'll call it Piranha.'

'Piranha?'

'Because of its teeth.'

My father inspected the pale preserve that passed for marmalade. 'I don't think that's a terribly good name for a dog,' he commented.

Again, I deferred to his judgment, asking if he had a better thought.

'Oh, I don't know. It's your dog, after all.' He took a sip of ersatz coffee. 'What about another piece of toast, old son?'

'Too long, Daddy.'

'Hm?'

I do not know who suggested 'Harris' but, so ludicrous was the contrast between the tiny scrap of black and white, and the mighty bomber chief, that the name immediately found favour. Then my mother offered, as I had hoped she would, to take charge of the orphan. 'Only until you're settled on a proper camp again,' she temporised, 'like you were at Wickenby.'

'That may take some time, Mummy. And you might want to keep him yourself by then. I mean, he is rather sweet, isn't he?'

'Of course, he is.' She glanced down at the puppy, by now sleeping soundly in her lap. 'But I think he's some sort of terrier, and I really only care for Pekes.'

My father, not entirely oblivious to the conversation, looked up from his second slice of toast. 'You think it may be a while before you're settled somewhere?'

'Probably, Daddy. If I live through this course, the next will be on gliders, then goodness knows what.'

'You didn't really want to fly gliders, darling,' said my

mother. 'Haven't you told somebody about that?'

I offered my father a cigarette. 'I've mentioned it, but I don't think anybody takes much notice.'

'You ought to jolly well make them take notice,' said Nina, firmly. 'I only married you because you were a bomber pilot.'

My father inspected the cigarette critically, and tapped one end on his thumbnail several times, before inserting the other end between his lips. I had often wanted to ask him why he did that. 'I expect they know what they're doing,' he observed. 'They probably want someone who can take charge when things go wrong – as you did sometimes on the Lancaster.'

Not for the first time in their wedded life, my mother did not see eye to eye with him. 'Nonsense, John,' she reasoned. 'They couldn't find anybody to fly their silly gliders, and they tricked him into it. He wants to fly a proper aeroplane.' She began to collect plates from the table, and Nina rose to help her. 'What I shall have to do,' said my mother, laying Harris in her last, lamented Pekinese's basket, 'is write to Mr Churchill.'

Nina watched her quizzically, wondering, perhaps, if she were serious. My father fetched an ashtray from the chimney-shelf and set it down between us. 'I'm not sure that you can expect him to interfere in Service matters of that sort,' he said. 'He's probably extremely busy.'

'Of course he is, John,' agreed my mother, 'but busy people are the ones who get things done. He wasn't too busy to arrange for your son to be a pilot, was he?' At the sink, she turned to Nina, who stood beside her with a drying-cloth. 'Jack was in the ARP, dear, driving ambulances, just to pass the time until he could get into the Air Force.'

My father took the cloth from Nina's hand. 'You must sit down and finish your coffee,' he directed. 'Drying the breakfast things is my job. Come along, now, young lady, I insist.'

'They said he was in a reserved occupation,' continued

my mother, 'and so they couldn't take him in. Mr Churchill soon made them change their minds of course.'

Nina glanced at me: I shrugged my shoulders. The effect was true enough, the cause I could not tell.

'Then again,' said my mother, busy with the dish-cloth, 'when he got to Wickenby and there weren't any library books, or ping-pong balls, or gramophone-records, and he couldn't buy any stamps…'

'Just a moment, Mummy,' I interrupted, 'who told you all that?'

'…and no YMCA, no Welfare Officer…who told me, dear? Well, I suppose you did yourself. Or it might have been one of the crew, when I was asking why you always had to take a taxi into Lincoln on your stand-downs and spend all your money in that hotel – what was it called? I wrote him a letter then.'

'The Saracen's Head. You never told me about this, Mummy.'

'It doesn't really matter what it was called. Hm? I'm telling you now, dear.' She passed a handful of wet knives and forks to my father. 'Put your cigarette out while you' re drying, please, John.'

'Yes, dear.' He turned to the ashtray, rolling his eyes resignedly at Nina.

'I had quite a nice letter back, from an Air Vice-Marshal Sanders – I expect Mr Churchill had spoken to him about it – except that he went on about what a splendid NAAFI there was at Wickenby and then rather spoiled it by saying that unfortunately the aircrew couldn't go there. But he did say they were going to make some changes in the Sergeants' Mess, and I think you did notice an improvement, didn't you, dear?'

'My commission came through about then, Mummy, so I can't really tell, but the other chaps said that things in the Mess got better as soon as I moved out. Of course, the officers reckoned that their Mess fell off a lot at the same time.'

Surprisingly, my father chuckled heartily at the slender

jest. It occurred to me that either I had misjudged him all those years, or that he was thinking of something else.

There was an element of humour in what happened the week after, back at Bridgnorth, but there were those of us who found it hard to see the joke. Captain Donovan, 'the roughneck' who concerned himself with ungentlemanly weapons, stood on the training ground, rocking gently on the balls of his feet, his close-cropped, mustard-coloured hair shining palely below the red beret. His sharply-moulded features strikingly resembled those of the movie actor, Jimmy Cagney, and his manner, too, was of the softly-spoken thug. His teaching methods were his own, and they had struck me as both simple and effective. I did not forget, as an example, his use of the mnemonic when teaching us the sequence of a simple battle briefing.

'Eleventh of May,' he had said, and chalked '11 MAI' upon the blackboard, 'written in the French way, like this. That's eye-eye-em-eh-eye, got it? First "eye" is information – go on, write it down, I shan't tell you again. That's when you inform your people about the general state of the battle – as much as they need to know about it, anyway. Second "eye" is intention – that's what you want them to do, what the purpose of the operation is. "Em" is for method – that's how they're going to do it, okay? The tactics, in other words…'

My third eye – imagination – had taken over. I had seen myself, crouched beneath the wing of the perfectly-positioned glider, somewhere far across the Rhine, with the eager, blackened faces of the airborne troopers turned towards me. 'Right, chaps,' I was quietly telling them, 'you see that fortress on the hill? It's supposed to be impregnable, but I don't think it is.' I had laughed, briefly, and heard the men's deep chuckle of response. 'Just give us the chance, sir,' growled someone from the darkness. 'That, Anstruther,' I replied, instantly recognising the burly corporal's voice, 'is exactly what I propose to do. Now, this is how we're going to knock it over…'

'"Eh" stands for administration,' Captain Donovan had continued, 'The usual back-up stuff – rations, ammo, transport, timings and so on. And the last "eye" is for intercommunication – lamp, radio, runner, whatever – call-signs and so on…'

Corporal Anstruther was cranking the generator-handle of the mobile RT set. I held the microphone against my lips. 'Hello, Anvil, this is Dagger. We're going in, I say again, we're going in, over.' Faintly through the headphones, I heard the voice from base. 'Roger, Dagger. Good luck, over.' I smiled, grimly, in the darkness. 'Thank you, Anvil, keep your fingers crossed for us. Over and out.'

'Are you listening to me, Flying Officer?' Captain Donovan had inquired. 'I don't like talking to my blasted self.'

'With you all the way, Captain. Eye-eye-em-eh-eye.'

'And then…?'

I had looked at him blankly.

'Dreaming, weren't you? Tell him, somebody.'

A fresh-faced Pilot Officer had given instant voice: 'Ask if there are any questions, sir.'

'And…?'

'Give a time-check, sir,' another sycophant had yelped.

'That is correct. Got it, Flying Officer?'

I had looked at him again, less blankly. 'I have been to a briefing or two before, Captain.'

'And given them,' Gittins had growled beside me.

The Captain had given us the thin-lipped Cagney grin. 'Yes, of course. "Target for Tonight", and all that stuff. Shall we get on?'

That had been last week. Now we were playing with mortars, in teams of three: one to pass the little bomb, one to drop it down the barrel, and a third to pull the trigger, while the first two stuck their fingers in their ears. As a weapon, it was probably more lethal than the bow-and-arrow, but not all that different to use: direction was decided by what your eyeball told you, and the range by simple trial and error.

When we had banged away at various targets for a happy half-an-hour or so, the Captain and his minions herded us together. 'Right, my hearties,' said the Captain, 'time for a spot of exercise. I want you over on that slope, the one with the copse above it, in three minutes from the off.' He pointed his forefinger like the barrel of a gun, at me. 'You're in command, Flying Officer.'

I brought them, panting, to a halt in the middle of the gently-rising field, and told them to relax. The morning mist had lifted, leaving glistening beads of water on the grass, to lie, a grey-blue film, between the meadow and the low-hung sun. In the copse above the field, the silver-birch-trees stood and let their last leaves drift away. All around was still and silent: no sound of distant train or car or aeroplane: no sound at all. The earth smelled old and dank. Squatting on my haunches, I took one of Archbold's cigarettes, and waited for what fate, and Captain Donovan, might bring.

Across the valley, on the firing-range, I saw the tiny figures of the Captain and his men, beside the mortars. Then, dampened by the distance and the moisture in the air, the detonations reached us – the noises that, when we were near, had made us stop our ears. The shells rose slowly – you could watch them all the way.

Gittins sprang to his feet with an agility I had not seen him demonstrate before. 'Bloody hell,' he commented, 'the bastards are firing at us!'

Reason said the Captain would not do that: instinct said he might. While I crouched and sought the synthesis of these emotions, the younger pilots, like cattle when you drive them from your path, ran clumsily, irrationally changing course, somehow missing a collision, heads turning over shoulders. My command was in disorderly retreat. Anstruther, where were you when I needed you?

Having reached their apogee, the shells began to fall, and I watched them with the utmost interest. Had the nearest been a hook-shot, and I at deep square leg, I would have had to run some thirty yards around the boundary to my right to catch it. Lowering my tin-hatted head in that direction, I pressed chin, chest and knees into the grass, and waited for the shattering explosion. None came. Drawing captions for a comic strip, you might have written 'crump', or possibly 'ker-plump'.

I raised my head and looked around. Archbold, it appeared, had accompanied the herd, no doubt to bring some order to their rout. Gittins, initially of like mind, had now returned to me, gasping blasphemies, 'They're not HE,' he reassured himself, 'They're sodding smoke-bombs.'

'Of course they are,' I said, as the clouds of vapour slowly billowed up, 'I'm surprised you didn't realise that.'

'Come off it, sport. You didn't bloody know.'

'You didn't think he'd really bomb us, did you?' Gittins was pulling his gas-mask from its bag. 'I wouldn't put it past him. Anyway, it wouldn't do much good if one of those buggers hit you on the bean.'

A loudhailer howled across the valley, through the drifting smoke. 'All right, my hearties, fun's over. Let's have you back here, on the double, come on, move!'

I looked round at the returning herd. 'Respirators on, gentlemen, and follow Mr Gittins. Hang on to the chap in front.'

I would have liked to ask the Captain what he purposed by the exercise, but by the time we reached the firing-range he and his NCOs had disappeared, leaving a hint of cordite only in the clammy air. And that final whiff, appropriately, was the last I knew of Captain Donovan, for next morning I was on my way to Shobdon, and the glider training school.

6

Glider Pilot

'**Y**ou'll have a little while to wait,' said the railwayman (who seemed to combine the functions of porter, ticket-collector and, for all I knew, of stationmaster, too). 'The stopping train's not due by here 'til six minutes past ten.' He peered up at me and gave a cheerful smile. 'That's if she's on time.'

I looked round for a clock, but the little station did not run to that facility, so I set one of my bags down on the platform and checked my wristwatch in the gloom. 'That's four hours, for heaven's sake!'

The railwayman took a heavy timepiece from his waistcoat pocket. 'Four hours and three minutes, sir. A pity it is there's no waiting-room. We're only what they call a halt, see, for the village people going to Leominster, mostly.'

'How far is it to the village?'

'No more than a step, sir. Not more than half a mile – well, not much more.'

'Is there a pub there?'

'A pub, sir?' He chuckled, dismissing the very notion of a publess village. 'I should hope so. Why, there's two good licensed houses there.'

'Thank goodness for that. If I could leave my bags here.'

'There's the Drover's Arms, and there's the Ram, sir. Open two nights a week, different nights, of course.'

Somehow I knew the answer before I asked the question. Neither the Drover's Arms, nor the Ram, would open their doors tonight. It had been that sort of day. A peripatetic crow, planning a route from Bridgnorth down to Shobdon, would have reckoned on less than thirty miles in flight. Travelling since early morning, I had already covered twice that distance, and still had ten more miles to go. I expressed my feelings in a word or two.

'There's language,' said the railwayman, tolerantly. 'Would it be your first visit to these parts, sir?'

I admitted that it was, and added the hope that it would also be my last. He muttered sympathetically, taking no offence, and consulted his great watch again. 'You're not ever so pleased at having to kick your heels for four hours, I can see. Now, if a bit of a sit-down in the warm would suit you, and a cup of tea...'

The railway cottage's sitting-room was of the same doll's-house dimensions as the halt itself, and the three of us (for the signalman had joined us) were all that it would comfortably hold.

'I couldn't help noticing that you're by way of being a pilot,' said the railwayman, tipping a stream of coke into the glowing fireplace. 'Is it fighters you are, or bombers?'

As we talked, I learned that the signalman's son flew in the turret of a Stirling, and that the stationmaster's favourite niece was in the WAAF. In turn, I confided that my recently-acquired father-in-law was himself a railwayman, albeit with the LMS. Time passed pleasantly. 'Mr Davies,' said the signalman, indicating his colleague with a nod, 'mentioned as to how you might have enjoyed a drink, if they'd been open.'

I could not deny that this was true, but protested that the tea was excellent.

'It'll be all the better,' the signalman suggested, producing a half-bottle of whisky from the pocket of his overcoat, 'for flavouring with this.'

As he liberally laced the steaming mugs, the memory of Eastoft came to mind, and of the landlord's wicked brother. But the signalman was absolutely right: whisky in hot, sweet tea was quite acceptable, while whisky in beer would never be. Later, we ate beans on toast and, warmed by this and by the whisky, I revealed my early wish to be an engine-driver – to thunder northwards on the footplate of the Coronation

Scot – before the sight of those great, droning Handley Pages at the Hendon air display had brought about a reappraisal. 'But I've always wanted,' I confessed, 'to travel in the driver's cab. That must be terrific fun.'

We had another cup of tea, similarly enlivened as the last. 'I think we might stop the through train, Alwyn,' said Mr Davies, 'I'm sure I can find an urgent package for Shobdon.' He turned to me. 'You'll have to cross the down-track, and climb up to the cab. Tell the driver that you've been with us. Tell him I don't want to trouble the guard about it. He's new to the line, bit of a stickler, you might say.'

The rushing passage through the night was all that I had hoped for, the cabin simple, serviceable and warm as I imagined. Smoke billowed past, the footplate pounded rhythmically and swayed beneath my feet. The faces of the driver and his fireman were a deep and vivid red, with the features darkly shadowed in the hot glow of the furnace. I took off my peaked cap and held my head out in the wind, as the fields of Hereford swept by. 'How fast,' I shouted, 'are we going now?'

'How fast do you think?'

'Sixty? Sixty-five?'

The driver chuckled. 'More like thirty. Give us a chance – the old girl's getting on a bit. And my mate's a cripple – idle with it an' all. Chuck some bloody coal on for the officer, eh, Fred?'

This was a chance no-one would want to miss, and I asked if I might undertake the stoking. 'You'll get your hands black,' counselled Fred, 'and your uniform I shouldn't wonder.'

'That's all right.'

The task, like other simple-seeming exercises – scything, rowing, felling trees or hitting golf-balls – was not so easy as it looked. 'I think I'd sooner have Fred,' observed the driver, when the sweat was running down my face, 'for all his faults. P'raps you'd do better at my job, seeing as you're a sort of driver. Catch hold of this handle for a minute. Keep it steady, where it is.'

I gave the shovel back to Fred, and sprang to realise the old ambition. Fighting down the urge to whoop with pleasure, and to turn my cap round back to front, I asked what it was you pulled to make the whistle blow. 'Never mind the whistle,' said the driver, 'you'll have the guard up here next stop to see what's going on.'

'Oh, come on,' I pleaded. 'Just one tiny whistle – I'll probably never get the chance again.'

He weakened, and I jerked the toggle. The wail swept past the cab into the night behind us, and we thundered on.

The toggle that I later learned to pull at Shobdon airfield made no sound. Silently, it opened up the hook and let the cable – the metal rope that tied the glider to the tug – fall as silently away. Pull that toggle, and your link with powered flight had gone. No energy, no sound – well, no more than the whisper of the slipstream and the merest creak of wooden members in the glider's fuselage. Now the force of gravity, inexorable enemy of every flying man since Icarus, must have its way. And that way – the only way – was down. Down, with no alternative, no stretching of the glide-path with a timely burst of throttle, no going round again if your approach was not quite right. Neither was the Hotspur one of your slender, sporting gliders, designed to play with rising draughts of air: it would not know a thermal if it saw one. The Airspeed people built it, like a baby version of their Oxford without engines, to be towed, released and landed – nothing more. Pull that toggle, nerve yourself, and know that what the apple showed to Newton was the truth.

On the take-off, you were airborne long before the tug, but you had to hold the glider down, not to fly too high above him, pulling up his tail, or he could never climb. Aloft, it did not matter where you put yourself, above him or below, high tow or low, so long as you kept station strictly aft. To fly at the same height as his was not a good idea, for there you would be riding in his slipstream, being buffeted and bounced in air made angry by his passage. There was nothing hard about the take-off – a normal child could do it – nor in ordinary flight, where all you had to do was fly formation, dead astern, without the sweat of holding station, for you had nowhere else to be but at the cable's length. Not quite so easy flying blind, with just the basic instruments, plus an extra one – the so-called 'angle of dangle' – that showed you where the cable was. The landing was simplicity itself: you merely scraped the underside along the grass and let the friction bring you to a halt.

The area where a sort of skill was needed lay in identifying the spot that you should land on and in making sure you did. This called for a little old-fashioned pilotage. You had to take into account your height and speed, the rate of your descent, and how much to allow for the prevailing wind. It took me back to Souther Field in Georgia, 1942, and made me grateful for the engine-off approaches, from all positions and directions, that the blessed Wallace Bacon Sheffield had insisted I perfect. At least to set the Hotspur down, right on the cross marked on the airfield, offered a small challenge, a counter-irritant to the pain of being reduced to flying this somewhat less than potent aircraft.

Meanwhile, the bombers' war went on without me: less against the long-range city targets I had known, more in the rôle of monstrous field artillery or naval guns, against the battle targets. So Walker, Protheroe and Fairbairn prospered on their second tours. 'Piece of piss, these days,' wrote Protheroe, combining the more usual 'piece of cake'; and 'easy as pissing' in a phrase, 'although some poor sods still seem to get the chop.' Cassidy, too, was back in action, navigating Lancasters from North Killingholme. His closest call had been when the Army truck in which he hitched a ride from Selby into York had chanced to meet a NAAFI van head-on. He had lost blood – 'paled like a ghost', he wrote, 'but kept my senses.' I would have backed him to do that.

Taking Nina to luncheon in the Strand, the paratrooper, Ivor Nelson, had revealed his love for Mary Halliday, her Harrow room-mate, and asked us both, Service exigencies permitting, to be present at their wedding. In a friendly reference to me, he had recalled our Halifax flight in Lincolnshire. 'Tell Jack,' he said, 'that when he beat up the pub on the Trent, it was the most terrifying moment of my life.'

The life of Douglas Sieffert, friend of the crew since Derby days at OTU, was less exciting. Lusting for adventure, after years in engineering draftsmanship, he had at last obtained an RAF commission, only to find himself behind another desk, as Technical Adjutant at Mildenhall. 'A pretty stoogy sort of job,' wrote Nina, sniffily (by her lights, men flew aeroplanes, women handled radar), 'for a chap of his experience. What's the mud like for crawling in at Shobdon? Any better than Bridgnorth? Hope the boils are better.'

It was my first experience of boils and, of all places, I had them in my ear. Cassidy, to whom an aviator's ears were as its nostrils to a hound, wrote darkly from North Killingholme, 'You want to watch your ears.' I did my best to watch them closely, and for a week the MO would not let me fly. Then there was a party in the No 1 Mess (all these training units seemed to tend towards apartheid between the students and the staff) and, to celebrate the healing of my boils, I took up one of the invitations – strictly limited to ten – which were extended to the lower orders.

Our reception at the function did not exactly warm the heart. 'Your bar is in this room, gentlemen,' announced a stone-faced orderly. 'There will be a small buffet at twenty-one hundred hours. You are requested not to use the other bars, which are reserved for senior officers, official guests and staff.'

A punch was served, in tiny spirit glasses. It tasted like cold tea. Left to ourselves, we shuffled feet and spoke in whispers. Pictures on the wall drew our attention: Mr Churchill, as grim as we were feeling, two haughty Air Chief Marshals, and several Welsh mountains, as bleak as our surroundings. A Flight Lieutenant entered, wearing a determined smile. 'Enjoying yourselves, chaps? That's the stuff – jolly good show.' Instantly, he disappeared.

Alf Gittins and I exchanged glances. 'I had more fun in sick quarters,' I said. 'As a matter of fact, I think I feel another boil coming on now – a pain in the neck, anyway.'

'Chap I feel sorry for,' said Gittins, 'is Archbold. He's missing all this, being duty dog.'

'I'm only waiting for the buffet then I'm off.' One of our juniors approached. 'Do you think it'd be all right if we circulated a bit? I mean, there is supposed to be a dance going on somewhere.'

Gittins frowned. 'You lecherous young monkey! Can't you think of anything but crumpet?'

The youngster grinned happily, and shook his head. Another put his oar in. 'Try and remember what you were like when you were young, Alf. Obviously, all you want now is a nice, quiet evening. but there must have been a time, when you had blood in your veins...'

Towering over his tormentor, Gittins took the bait. Far from falling off with age, he vehemently declared, his sexual proclivities were stronger now than ever. Furthermore, his potency and vast experience had made him more desired of women than Valentino in his prime. 'They queue up for it, mate, down Bethnal Green, when the word gets out I'm home on leave. I have to fight them off.'

'Righty-ho, then, Alf, let's see you do your stuff. Get 'em lined up on the dance floor.'

'Crumpet! Christ, I've had more crumpet than you lot have had hot dinners. And I'll still be having it, when you're all in bloody bathchairs.' The young men led him, boasting still, but with decreasing cogency, out of the room.

One glance told me that the dance was not for us. The girls – WAAF and WRAC officers with a sprinkling of nursing sisters – had long since been claimed. Their escorts looked upon us coldly. Gittins, baffled but not beaten, suggested an 'excuse-me' to the leader of the band, who shook his head. I left them standing in a corner, forlornly watching the uncaring dancers. Walking down a corridor, and hearing voices raised in cheerful conversation, I paused beside a door, walked on, then stopped and reconsidered. After all, I was invited to their party. At my entrance, the tide of conversation ebbed away, and I walked up to the bar in silence. I asked for beer.

'Pint, sir?'

'May I have your bar-book number, sir?'

'I haven't got a bar-book. I'm a guest.'

'Of course, sir.' I noticed that he had not pulled the pint. 'Official or private, sir?'

'Blowed if I know. Official, I suppose – I'm from the other Mess.'

The barman's manner underwent a subtle change – a certain diminution of civility. 'Number Two Mess, sir? Your room's down the corridor, third on the left.'

'I don't like it there. It's all right, I'll pay cash.'

'Sorry, sir. We haven't any facilities for cash.'

Gary Cooper, similarly placed, would have smiled his slow, quiet smile and reached across the counter for a bottle. With an effort, I contrived the smile, but my arm was not so long as Gary Cooper's. The barman backed away a little. He probably had a shotgun hidden somewhere close at hand. I beckoned to him. 'A beer, please, steward. I'm a guest at this damn party, and I would like a beer. If you can't give me one, find somebody who can.' It did not come up to Gary Cooper's style, but it was the best that I could do.

'Perhaps you'd like to see the PMC, sir.'

'I'll see anybody who pours beer.'

The barman's eyes flickered round the room. Safe from the shotgun while his hands were still in sight, I, too, took a look around. Stiff, affronted stares were hastily averted. Clearly, strangers were unwelcome in this joint. I decided that I had to break the ice. 'Good evening, gentlemen. Thanks for inviting me to your lovely party. Anybody like a beer?'

Among the hostile mutterings, I heard somebody say 'For God's sake, give the bloody man a drink. Perhaps he'll bugger off.' An officer detached himself from one of the groups and came towards me. I recognised the Flight Lieutenant who, two weeks before, had introduced me to the Hotspur. He nodded to the barman. 'That's all right, steward. Put it on my book.' He looked at me anxiously. 'You're not really supposed to be here, you know. Bit embarrassing.'

'It is, isn't it? Cheers.'

'I heard you'd been off sick. All right, now?'

'Fit to fly tomorrow.'

'Good show.'

He looked at me warily, head down, and shifted his weight from foot to foot.

'You don't have to stay with me,' I said, 'I'll be perfectly happy on my own.'

'It's not that, old boy. Trouble is, you see...' He broke off as a Squadron Leader sauntered up, a thumb between the top two buttons of his tunic, tankard dangling from the forefinger. 'I say, Burrowes,' he drawled, 'is this chap your guest?'

On the defensive, my pint-provider sought a socially acceptable position. 'Oh, no, sir. Not at all. Well – not exactly. Actually, you see, sir, I sent him solo on the Hotspur, so...'

I sprang to his assistance. 'I'm sorry, sir, I didn't catch your name?'

The tankard-dangler's eyes threw hostile sparks in my direction. 'Probert,' he barked. 'Squadron Leader Probert. And what might yours be?'

Deep down inside, a glow suffused my heart. Who said that music hall was dead? 'Very decent of you, sir' I emptied the glass and passed it to the barman. 'Another pint, please, steward. On Squadron Leader Probert's book.'

Automatically, the barman filled the glass. All he needed, when the night was ended, was a bar-book entry, to balance dispensations against stock. Squadron Leader Probert, on the other hand, with colleagues' eyes upon him, had matters of prestige at stake. Red-cheeked, he banged his tankard on the bar and faced me squarely, searching for the blistering phrases that would put me in my place. As yet, like Lear, he knew not what they were, but when he found them, they would be the terror of the earth.

Luckily for me, and for the earth, fate intervened, in the shape of simple, mundane happenings. First, the robot barman filled the Squadron Leader's tankard and, while he was about it, the Flight Lieutenant's too. While Probert, purpling, watched this piling up of injury on insult, came the second happening. This was Gittins, with whom no one could compete for mundaneness, lurching through the sacred door, and peering thirstily about. Looking at the man, in the context of that well-tailored company, it occurred to me that either he had put on height and weight since his commissioning, or that his uniform had shrunk. Whatever the reason might have been, the result, if not grotesque, was not entirely svelte. Nevertheless, he was my colleague and, as compared with those about, my friend. 'Over here, Alf,' I called, and nodded to the barman. Probert's frown was terrible to see. 'This, sir,' I explained, 'is another of your guests. His name…'

'There you are, you bastard,' cried Gittins, jovially, 'we've been looking all over the bloody place…' He, flung the door wide open. 'All right, you chaps, in here!'

As the party sidled in behind him, eight more obviously thirsty officers, the full horror of the situation dawned on Squadron Leader Probert. He leaned across the bar. 'Official guests, steward,' he hissed, 'all these people. On the Guests' Book, understand?'

They fell upon the beer with happy cries. No 1 Mess, they agreed, was not such a bad place, after all, and Probert, stifling his feelings, acknowledged calls of 'Cheerioh, sir' with a gracious nod. But to my brooding mood, the atmosphere seemed hostile still. No friendly glance came from the company: smooth, barathea-clad backs were turned away. More haughty Marshals sneered down from the walls, more frozen landscapes, an astonished stag. Even George VI's features looked unnaturally stiff: only the portrait of his Queen held any semblance of humanity and warmth.

Gittins, refreshed, undid the straining buttons of his tunic (at which Probert turned away as from an obscene act), and brushed a speck of froth from his moustache. 'That's better,' he admitted, 'but, Christ, these buggers haven't a clue how to run a Mess do, have they? I've seen better parties in the YM at Mildenhall, blowed if I haven't.'

'Why is it, Alf,' I asked him, 'that nobody likes us here? I mean, what's wrong with us?'

A finger pushed against my arm, and I turned to look into the angry, bloodshot eyes of a stocky Flying Officer, wearing an air-gunner's badge and the ribbon of the 1939-43 Star. A quiff of hair was combed across his forehead, like a horizontal question-mark, and a short, tobacco-stained moustache bristled as though it had a savage answer to the quiff. 'I can tell you why the sods don't like you, Jack,' he rasped.

I asked him how he knew my name.

'I don't – I just call everybody Jack. Everybody bar the CO.'

'What do you call him?'

'Nothing. I've never met him – never even met the bastard. That's the sort of place this is, Jack.' He transferred a half-full glass to his left hand, and held out his right. 'I'm Doc,' he said.

Gittins, who had been slowly sipping beer and gaping round the room in his best village-idiot style, now looked down at the Flying Officer with a semblance of interest; 'Are you the MO, then?'

'Course not. Name's Docherty – known as Doc, Jack.'

'I'm Alf,' said Gittins, who clearly had not paid attention, 'he's Jack.'

'You were going to tell us,' I pursued, 'why we're so unpopular.'

'Don't you worry, Jack, they hate me too. Tell you what, if they didn't, that's when you want to start worrying. It'd worry me. Let the sods hate me – I'd rather.'

'Yes, but why?'

He jerked his head at Probert's back. 'That bastard's typical. Spent five years keeping out of the war, he has. Made a career of it. Squadron Leader? Bollocks. They're all the same, Jack. The anti-fighting air force – conchies in uniform.'

Gittins took another slow gape round the room. 'And that makes them anti-us, does it?'

'Chairborne warriors, instructors, the bullshit brigade – I've shat 'em, Jack. They can't stand the sight of us. 'Cause we're the boys, aren't we? Operational. Been there, Jack – been there and back. They know it, and they can't bloody stand it.'

Our charges had settled to a game of Liar Dice, oblivious and uncaring of the revelations we were hearing. Gittins drained his glass and set it on the bar. 'What were you on, then, Doc?'

'Halibags. The good old Halibag, on 51 at Snaith. Tail-gunner in Bob Slater's crew. Christ, he was a mad bastard, old Bob – bloody good pilot. Know him, did you, Jack?'

'He's Jack,' Gittins insisted. 'I was on Stirlings. He was on Lancs.'

Docherty looked disappointed: everyone should have known his pilot. 'Yeah. Thought you might have met him on training, or something. Bloody good type.'

'Did a tour with him, did you, Doc?'

'We were a team in that crew, Jack. Well, you had to be, then. And parties! Christ! I tell you what, I'd like to see old Bob Slater walk through that…' Waving a hand towards the door, he noticed that his glass was empty.

'Here, you're on Mess Guests, aren't you? Put me one in when you get yours, go on. I'll do the sods for a pint, anyway, the sods.'

Summoned, the barman shrugged disdainfully and

poured the drinks. Gittins cocked a heavy eyebrow at Docherty and, relentlessly, resumed his inquisition. 'How many did you do, then, with this famous crew?'

'Eh? Oh, I don't know. Fourteen or fifteen, I can't remember. I got this bloody sinus trouble, Jack. The bloody MO...well, you know how it is with sinus.'

'I'm Alf,' said Gittins, 'and you're a scrounging little squit. Take your drink and piss off.'

The quiff was more questioning than ever, the moustache more bristling. 'Here, you can't talk...'

I put the glass into his hand. 'Alf has to be careful with his health,' I said, 'at his age. He's afraid your sinus might be catching. Goodnight, Doc.'

Hot eyes flickering, he backed away, but no further than the dice-playing glider-pilots. His missionary zeal, I realised, was not exhausted yet. Gittins's slow gaze came back to me. 'Sinus isn't catching,' he observed.

'I just said that to make him feel better. You were so bloody rude.'

'Well, I didn't like him. And his breath stank.'

There seemed to be an epidemic of not liking people at that Station. I had a sudden picture in my mind of Nina – soft and caring, warm to touch and sweet of breath. It had been her twenty-third birthday on 14th November, and it would be mine next week. Writing to thank me for my telegram, she had sent her London news. No more doodle-bugs, now that the Allied armies' eastward march had taken out their launching-sites, but still the rockets sometimes woke her in the night. Mary Halliday and she had sworn that each could hear the beating of the other's heart, when one had fallen close enough to shake the soot into the fireplace. There were few military chores, compared with Station life, but she had served her turn in charge of pay parade, the only ritual to which the town-based WAAFs were called, when, once a fortnight, with all pleats pressed and buttons shining, prim unpainted mouths where butter would not melt, and not a lock of hair in contact with the collar, they marched up to the table, intoned the last three digits of their Service number, and received the royal wages of an airwoman's war. 'You can buy me a pint,' Nina's Wing Commander had said, 'with any money over. Any under, of course, you make up yourself.'

She had monitored the puppy's progress – 'very sweet but rather naughty' – on calls at Whitmore Road, from which, if night had fallen, my father would escort her to her door. 'He always says it's what you would do, if you were here.' And beyond your door, I thought, my darling Nina. So strange a state of marriage: two hundred miles apart, seldom meeting, and then rarely alone. No worse, I knew, than tens of thousands more such couples, all across the world, but none the more acceptable for that. And I had begun to tease myself with strange, unfounded fears: I, whose confidence and self-conceit had been a by-word, now fidgeted and fretted at the thought of Nina, so ripe, so vulnerable, so available, to all the stallions in London. It seemed quite likely that a normal, healthy girl, once aroused, might, for the pleasure that she knew it gave her, accept the sort of sexual advance (and there was never any lack of these, as I should be aware) which, hitherto, propriety and the fear of the unknown had conditioned her to parry. The streets of town, the whole world knew, were crowded with unprincipled philanderers – scented Poles, opulent Americans, rampant Australians, even my own importunate compatriots – all ravening to possess her. Had not Errol Magnus, smooth, sophisticated Errol, taken her to dinner at the Dorchester? She, herself, had freely told me so. Had he then politely seen her to her tube-train? That would not have been the Errol that I knew. And this fantasy of Ivor Nelson, taking her out to plead his love for Mary – a typical behind-the-lines tactic, now I came to think about it, from the handsome paratrooper. And her story of the *Evening Standard* van-driver, who had come so kindly to her rescue when she had missed the last bus home – well, really! I had been a van-driver myself, and

I knew their wicked ways with girls to whom they gave lifts.

These prickings only seemed to come with drink, as though the alcohol released some latent bubbles of self-doubt and insecurity. Had 'Othello' been one of the works that I was made to read at school, I might have recognised the syndrome, and seen the added twist that, as the Moor, I was playing Iago to myself.

As I took the cigarette that Gittins offered, and another look around that hostile room, an atavistic Celtic gloom swept over me. Friendless, poor and hungry, recently the victim of a vile infection, probably betrayed, and certainly condemned to fearful battle with the Wehrmacht in the nearest future, I felt a deep and bitter sorrow for myself. 'I can't understand you,' I told Gittins, 'the only chap who's tried to be decent to us in the whole damn place, at least made the effort to talk to us, and you treat him like that.'

Gittins was entirely unrepentant. 'I know the type, mate. Got a bloody great chip on his shoulder, and tries to put it on yours. I don't want his chip, or his sinus, or his breath, and that's all there is to it.'

In a dimly-lighted corner, a leg was nonchalantly draped across the armrest of a chair, while its owner held discourse with two or three other companions. Suddenly that leg, the trouser so well-pressed, the shoe so elegantly polished, seemed to cry out for a hot foot. Gittins, making much of stubbing out his cigarette in the party's ashtray, provided cover as I introduced a matchstick between the sole and upper of the splendid shoe, lit it, and retired like Zinzindorff's opponent in my current favourite story, in dignity and silence to the bar.

Gittins took his glass up, and glanced across his shoulder. 'Bloody thing's gone out,' he complained.

'No, it hasn't. He'll feel it in a moment. Pay no attention, and remember, it's nothing to do with us, or there'll be no more free beer. And where's that blasted buffet?'

Catching the word, the dice-players left their game and

gathered round us. One or two made suggestive, slavering noises, but now my thoughts had turned to Zinzindorff. 'Feeling the need of liquid refreshment,' I began, 'I retired to the nearest hostelry, where I happened to meet a fellow who offered to buy me a drink...'

A voice from the corner rose in horrified expostulation. 'I say, my damn shoe's on fire! I say, that's jolly rum!'

'...Naturally, I accepted. During the course of conversation, I chanced to mention that I'd killed a man. "Killed a man?" he said. "Yes," I said. "Good Lord," he said, "what was his name?" "Zinzindorff," I said. "Zinzindorff?" said he, "how do you spell that?"'

In the corner, the shoe had been removed, and was being feebly fanned by its owner. 'Honestly,' he was saying, more in sorrow than in anger, 'I've never known anything like this happen in the Mess before. Somebody's idea of a practical joke, I suppose...'

'"Zed aye enn-zin, zed aye enn-zin, dee ah ah double eff-dorff: Zinzindorff," I said. "Sir" he said, "you have killed my brother." We repaired to the field of honour...'

(At this point, Gittins and I stood back to back and, poker-faced, acted out the subsequent charade.)

'...We paced, we turned, we fired: he fell dead.'

Gittins, with that native gift for histrionic expression that so frequently lies dormant in the English race, now clutched his breast, gasped, swayed, and fell, like a dynamited chimney-stack. The smoking shoe no longer had the room's entire attention.

'Feeling the need of liquid refreshment,' I continued, nodding to the barman, 'I retired to the nearest hostelry, where I happened to meet a fellow who offered to buy me a drink. Naturally, I accepted. During the course of conversation, I chanced to mention that I had killed a man...'

One of the brighter members of our group was quick to seize the chance of playing a speaking part. 'Killed a man?' he said.

'Yes,' I said.

'Good Lord! What was his name?'

'Zinzindorff.'

'Zinzindorff? How do you spell it?'

'Zed aye enn-zin, zed aye enn-zin, dee oh ah double eff-dorff: Zinzindorff.'

'You cad, sir,' he roared (building up the part a little), 'you have killed my brother!'

More pacing, turning and firing followed. As the budding Gielguds took their roles, each striving to outdo the last in the drama of his dying, the floor became more thickly carpeted with writhing, groaning bodies, and Zinzindorff had several brothers left, still ripe for vengeance, when an exodus of officers, muttering about the long-awaited buffet, tempted the actors from the stage, and closed the show. Docherty, the last to leave, paused at the door and beckoned me to join him. 'Grub up, Jack,' he called, 'come and get it!'

I shook my head, and turned back to the bar. Patiently, the barman filled my glass. 'Aren't you going to partake of the buffet, then, sir?'

'Can't be bothered – there'll be an awful scrum.'

The barman nodded. Although the room was quite deserted, he leaned across the bar, glancing left and right, and addressed me in a whisper. 'Best have a bite inside you, sir. You sit yourself down by the fire, and I'll get you something from round the back, when I get me own.'

People, I mused, warming my bottom under George VI's disinterested gaze, were unpredictable. Not only that, but you never knew what they might do next. In half-an-hour, that barman's snootiness had altered to a sort of prim solicitude; the man who would have sent me slinking from the room into the outer darkness, now killed whatever fatted calf lay hidden in the kitchens 'round the back'. Nor were people, when you came to think about it, always what, on first acquaintance, they might seem to be. Gittins, for example, amiable, gregarious, as you would have thought, had suddenly revealed a harsh malevolence. Burrowes, too, so free and easy in the cockpit of the glider, had grown stiff with social inhibitions in his Mess.

And life's events, the march of things, were just as unpredictable. Taking my case: the bomber tour, followed by the so-called rest, and then another tour, that would have been the natural progression, if anything were natural in war. Yet here I was, a stranger in a world of khaki, because some drink-befuddled staff officer had not told the truth.

The more I thought of it, munching the collation that the barman brought, the more it seemed that I had walked through life as though the path were always firm, and the direction straight ahead, whereas, in fact, I walked on shifting sands, towards a goal that fate, or someone else, selected: certainly, not I. There seemed to be no pattern, nothing to rely on. I remembered that my little sister, at the pictures, would whisper in my ear, as each new character appeared: 'Is he decent or rotten?' Like me, she sought to have the record straight, to know that black and white were well-defined, to know the truth.

But what was the truth? Beauty, said John Keats; and beauty, truth. I would have liked to argue that with Keats. 'That's all very well, Keats,' I would have said, 'but didn't somebody point out (or will, Keats – I'm not quite sure about your dates) that beauty lies in the eye of the beholder? See what I mean, Keats? You and I might behold beauty quite differently. And, by your thesis, the same thing goes for truth.'

'No, as a matter of fact,' I would have continued (when you got the chance to talk things over with a chap like Keats, you might as well make the most of it), 'truth isn't necessarily beautiful at all – haven't you ever heard of 'the plain truth'? It can be pretty ugly, actually, if you'll excuse the paradox.'

I put the tray down on the floor, and settled back into the chair. I had to say this for Keats, he was a super chap to talk to. 'And I'll tell you another thing: people just don't tell the truth. Beautiful people, people who love you, even. You must have noticed that, Keats. They tell you downright lies, sometimes. They used to tell me that I'd get appendicitis if I swallowed cherrystones, or grapepips, or things like that. Frightened me for years. Did they ever tell you that, Keats? And cigarettes stunted your growth – absolute rot. I know lots of enormous chaps who smoke like furnace chimneys.' Perhaps that was not the happiest of thoughts: Keats, now that I came to look at him, was rather on the small side. 'Did you smoke a lot, yourself, Keats? Never mind, I'll give you another instance: they said you'd go blind if you abused yourself. Well! You wouldn't know Wank Hancox, but he was at my school. Do you know what he is now? Ace fighter pilot, Keats, Hawk-eye Hancox, they call him, these days. Now, if you'd said "Truth is what someone wants you to believe, and beauty is what you want to believe…"'

I gathered that Keats was saying something about Hellenic classicism, and the essential message of the urn, when Gittins shook me rudely by the shoulder.

'Wakey-wakey, you dozey man,' he rasped, with horrid heartiness, 'don't you know there's a war on? I just got the whisper, in the buffet with the toffs – we're off to Brize bloody Norton next week. Horsas, mate – sodding great gliders and thousands of squaddies.' He pulled the pin from an imaginary grenade with his teeth, and lobbed it down the room. 'Watch out, Rommel! Watch out, Von bloody Runstedt, Alf's coming!'

I wished Keats had still been there: Gittins was a fact, all right, his presence and his words were particles of truth. But to find the beauty in them at that moment was more than I could do.

7

Night Flying on Mosquitoes

I levelled the Mosquito out at twenty-thousand feet, and gently tipped the right wing down. The lumps and hollows of the Cotswolds swung slowly round the long, smooth cowling of the starboard Merlin. A hundred miles away, a misty, blue horizon crawled obliquely past the nose. A touch more on the rudder, a little backward pressure on the stick, and the banking angle steepened. Beyond the navigator's shoulder, the town of Banbury appeared, the Cherwell running South to Oxford's great, grey halls, the tiny, moated Broughton Castle, and Blenheim Palace with its shining lake. Down there, somewhere, were the airfields where my new adventure lay: solid, peacetime-built Upper Heyford, and its grimly-hutted satellite with the deceptively attractive name of Barford St John.

To reach this altitude, a laden Lancaster would have been climbing for an hour or more: the Mosquito needed just ten minutes. Events since P Staff snatched me from Brize Norton seemed to have moved almost as fast.

Not ungratefully, I had handed in the pistol, boots and khaki to the stores, and taken train for London. 'Don't ask me why, old boy,' the Air House officer had drawled, looking up serenely from his sixth-floor desk in Kingsway. 'Apparently, they want you back in Bomber Command.'

He had flicked open the cover of a file, and picked up his spectacles. Even upside-down, I had recognised the writing on the topmost paper. Across it, someone had scrawled a phrase in bright, green ink.

'It seems that your glider posting was some sort of clerical error...'

There was something slightly dotty, and deeply reassuring, about a country whose every last resource was bent to total war, in which a mother's voice, raised in the interests, as she saw them, of her son, could still be heard within the corridors of high command, no matter of what

111

minimal significance those interests might be.

'What about Gittins,' I had asked, 'and Archbold?'

'Who?'

The sixth floor had known nothing of my colleagues, and cared little more. In the ever-changing pattern of calculated accidents that was Service life in war, our paths had crossed, and parted: that was that. Good luck, chaps, and don't forget the safety-catch.

'Point is,' the Kingsway potentate had said, 'where are we going to post you?'

I had boggled at him. If he really wanted a suggestion, the Bahamas came immediately to mind, a nice, quiet Air Attaché's post, or, better still, an indefinite spell of leave. 'I used to think,' I muttered, 'that I was indecisive. Now, I'm not so sure.'

I had remembered his remark – Bomber Command were calling. 'What about Wickenby – 626 or 12?'

'Can't send you straight to a Squadron – out of the question.' He had turned a paper over on the file. 'You're a QFI, I see, multi-engined; presumably that's what they want you for. You'd better go to an HCU – any preference?'

That was how I had returned to Blyton, to the bosom of Gp Capt Nelson, of Spiller, Woody and the rest, back to exactly where I was six months before – well, not quite exactly, for then I was a bachelor, without responsibility, without a thought for any but myself. All that had changed – at least, it should have changed. The fact, however, was that simply reading 'Darling Husband' in a letter, instead of 'Darling Jack', had not entirely changed my life. To be really married, and to feel you were, took rather more than that. You had to be together, night and morning, take turns in the bathroom, pass the marmalade, share the clothing coupons. All we had so far was a status, not a marriage. The case matched, in a way, that of the dog – the pocket Harris, also far away, for whom I did not have to raise a hand; mine in name but not in fact.

Blyton, too, had changed, in several aspects. Only two or three Australians remained: the rest had either gone, like Cassidy, to rejoin bomber squadrons, or sailed for home, to fight the war on their own doorstep, with the Japanese; Crummy, too, had gone, to command the base at Lindholme; most strikingly, no Halifaxes stood on the dispersals.

'Yes, we've re-equipped,' said Spiller. 'Perhaps you won't be quite so bolshie, flying the Lanc.'

Almost a year had passed since I had clambered up to the familiar cabin and swung myself into that lofty seat. A year, since Wickenby, of awkward Oxfords, heavy Halifaxes, humble Hotspurs; and now, at last, the 'big, black beaut' again, the Queen. I had tingled as the Merlins cleared their throats to drone the overture, and joined them, singing, as their chorus mounted to the sky. The memories had flooded over me with every movement, every movement had brought back the sense of balance, symmetry and power.

Cloud had lain across the fields of Lincolnshire, base four hundred feet at best; I had settled to the instruments as my mother to her piano music-rack, and let the aeroplane climb smoothly through the sight-denying mist. Teasingly, the murk had sometimes lightened for a moment, and turned to grey opacity again, while the airscrews sliced through flashing swathes of vapour, and the engines' beat was echoed from the cloud. At last, the fuselage had breasted through the topmost, floating billows and swum slowly, strongly, into the stinging blueness of the empty sky above. Soft fingers had reached up to touch the aircraft, clinging like a woman loath to let her lover go, then, white and silent, falling back, knowing that in time he must return. Meanwhile, the sky was mine.

Then, climbing in that unpurposed Lancaster, bombless and unarmed, the thought had come to me of Cassidy, not thirty miles away, and halfway through a second squadron life. He had a purpose. I had thought of Protheroe and Fairbairn, both in the battle still; and Walker, not satisfied with twenty operations for his tour on PFF, but begging missions with a USAF squadron at the waist-gun of a Fortress. I had thought of all the crew of Charlie Two at Wickenby, and deeply wished that they were in that aircraft, flying with me.

But they were not, and I had known by then that they never would be, not again. The war was not a nice, team game for me to play, nor was the Air Force run by sentimental men. Bill Spiller knew that, too, and he had told me so before. At least, I had the Lancaster, and I made the most of her that high, blue morning: corkscrew patterns in the sky, steep banking dives, abrupt enough to lift me off the seat, and climbing turns that pressed my chin into my chest. Then, a little flap, the Merlins throttled back, down through the cloud again along a radar lattice-line, until the flat fields of the Isle of Axholme had come darkly into sight.

'We've just passed over Hatfield Woodhouse,' the engineer had said. 'Ever been to "The Green Tree" there, skip? Nice little pub … Cripes, look at that!'

'What? Where?'

'Lindholme, starboard beam. Hangar's on fire – the one by Flying Control!'

I had tipped the wing and made a circuit of the base, watching flames and densely-rolling smoke, the urgent gathering of trucks, the tiny figures of the airmen moving helter-skelter to the scene. Then the well-remembered Vauxhall had come across the tarmac like a dart, full speed from SHQ, and slithered to a halt. Even at three hundred feet, I had fancied that I smelt the scorching tyres and heard the car-door slam. The engineer had raised eyebrows as I laughed aloud. 'I'm just imagining old Crummy,' I had told him, 'he'll be tearing people apart down there – he'll probably court-marshal the CTO for arson.' It had been a happy picture to take with me, of Crummy, so languid of deportment but so blistering of tongue, fighting fire with fire, as the Lancaster swept back below the overcast to Blyton.

For the ensuing seven days, my feet had seldom touched

the ground – Spiller had seen to that. My pupils learned to fly the Lancaster by morning, afternoon and night. Even a large, lugubrious Pole who spoke no English – none at all – had mastered the rudiments sufficiently to go into the air alone after three hours of the well-tried sign-and-wrist-slap language in the circuit. Then, sitting at lunch with Wood and Spiller, the march of events had taken yet another turn. Those of us who, commissioned in the RAFVR 'for the duration of the present emergency', had no particular idea of what to do if we survived, had been recently encouraged to apply for regular commissions, and the application forms had now arrived for our completion. Woody, in the intervals between sucks of soup through the filter of his wing-commanderly moustache, was passing comment.

'Can't say I like answering all these damn questions about myself. I mean, the more the buggers know about a chap, the less likely they are to take him on. Are you applying, Spiller?'

The Flight Commander, fastidiously breaking small, grey chunks of bread into his plate, had given a wintry smile. 'Probably not, sir.'

'Course not. You'll be going back to that solicitor's office in Cambridge, or wherever it is, to make a fortune, I expect. It's all right for chaps like you, with qualifications.'

I had tried to make him feel better about it. 'I'm applying, sir.'

'Are you really? You'll probably get it, too.' He had paused as the waitress changed his plate. 'Not sure I want to be in an Air Force that would have an awkward young sod like you as a regular officer.'

'Thanks very much, sir. I knew I could rely on you for a good recommendation.'

He had stuck the corner of a napkin more securely into the neck of his blouse and a fork into the shepherd's pie. 'Tell you what I will do, though. I'll let you have my Mossie posting.'

I had swallowed hard and coughed, as a piece of carrot,

taken by surprise, mistook the windpipe for the gullet. 'Excuse me. Would you mind saying that again, sir?'

'A posting came through this morning, for Upper Heyford, the Mossie OTU. I was going to take it myself, but… well, do you want it or don't you?'

I pointed the Mosquito's nose north-east, and settled snugly in the seat. 'Let's pop up to Lincolnshire,' I suggested to the navigator, 'and make a pass over one or two of my old bases.'

Sgt Dixon's pallid, pleasant face, close beside my shoulder in the narrow cockpit, took on a worried look. 'I don't think I've got the charts for Lincolnshire, skipper – I thought we were just on local flying…'

At least he had not called me 'sir'; that had taken some persistence to achieve. 'You won't need the radar, Dicky. Once we pick up the Trent, I know every blade of grass by its Christian name.'

'Oh – right-ho, skipper.'

'Mind you, you'll have to navigate me back…'

Upper Heyford had been a revelation. It was as though the colleges of nearby Oxford had reached out and touched its paths with elegance, its walls with dusky red and ancient, clinging ivy. After the noisy training-grounds of Shobdon, the hostile air of Bridgnorth, and Blyton's freezing sheds of corrugated iron, it was another, and a more salubrious, world at Upper Heyford. For the first time since I left my father's house to join the Royal Air Force, I had a room – a fine room – to myself, in a cosy, pre-war OMQ And I had a servant – such a servant! Not a hurried, temperamental WAAF, but a male civilian, who had grown old in the service of far greater men than I. So venerable and dignified was Partington that my instinct was to open doors for him, to help him with his chores.

But that would not have done, for it seemed to be his pleasure to treat me like his favourite in a lengthy line of lords. 'When I came in from night-flying, I had written to my mother, "Partington was waiting with fruit salad, cakes and cream. And the previous two nights he fed me with hard-boiled egg sandwiches, Cornish pasty and mince-tart. Wish I could take him with me when I leave here.'

'I say, Partington,' I had commented one evening, toying with the cheese and biscuits while he hung my tunic in the wardrobe.

'Yes, sir?'

'Where the devil do you get all this stuff from – all this super grub?'

He had smiled benignly. 'I like to see a young gentleman with a good appetite. If you'll excuse me for mentioning it, sir, your second pair of shoes are a little worn at the heel. With your permission, I'll have them seen to.'

'Please do. But the grub, Partington… I mean, people in palaces aren't doing as well as this.'

He had turned the sheet back on my bed. 'Ways and means, sir, ways and means. Would there be anything further, sir?'

'No, thanks, Partington.'

'Possibly a cup of cocoa for a nightcap?'

Did Bertie Wooster ever have it quite so good?

At a steady 300 mph, well throttled back, the Mosquito passed over Leicestershire in a long, descending arc. Dixon had put aside the Gee-box and, having drawn a careful pencil-line from Barford up to Lincoln on the quarter-million chart, was practising his map-reading. Glancing at the heavy features, wholly concentrated on his task, I tried to picture him on operations, far out over Germany, in the depth of night and heaps of trouble. How would he react, when I told him that an engine would not run, controls were solid, iced, and that my piles were killing me? Not, perhaps, like Cassidy – 'aw, cripes, don't give us the horrors, Jack' – for he was not that kind of man.

All the pilots on the course had flown operations of

some sort or another, either overseas or in the European theatre, but only two of the navigators had any such experience. The remainder, twelve young sergeants, had shown some aptitude in training, and so had found themselves at Upper Heyford, assigned to navigate the 'wooden wonder', in which things happened half as fast again as in the heavy bombers. I had flown with several of these likely lads in Oxfords, on cross-countries out of Heyford, on practice bombing-runs, and juggling with the beam. They were capable, and conscientious, and all that anyone could ask for reckoning a course, and yet there was not one of whom I felt that I should clasp to my heart with hoops of steel. Gradually, however, Dixon had appeared beside me in the cockpit more than others, and at Barford on the Mossies, I had flown with none but him.

'Do you,' my mother had written to enquire, 'know any of the pilots on your course? Do you like them?' That was always her first question about any new acquaintance – 'do you like him?' Often it confused me, for the thought of liking or not liking seldom came into my mind. Chaps were there, they were themselves, and that was that. It was hard to think of any whom I actively disliked, but that was not to say I really liked them. What did 'liking' mean? Bacon and eggs for breakfast, yes, I liked; the feel of linen on the skin; the smell of linseed oil, or coffee; Nina's cheek on mine; great branches moving in the wind; a starlit sky on summer nights; there were so many favourite things, things that I could say I liked.

But with people, you would not make so positive a judgement. You might find this trait or that congenial, if you came to think about it, and another not; you might enjoy a fellow's sense of humour one day, find it tiresome on the next; you could admire his choice of words, the way he spoke, but wish, another time, he would not talk so much. A better way to measure what you thought of people, I would have argued with my mother, was to reckon what dislikes and likes you had in common. Perhaps that was her meaning, perhaps her words were verbal shorthand.

'As to the other pilots on the course,' I had replied, 'the only one I know is Tony Wright, who was at Wickenby, but they seem a pretty decent bunch.'

This fulsomeness was not entirely out of place. After all, they were all men whose mettle had been proved, to some extent. Their characters were formed, for good or ill, and were their own. Pearce, for instance, so fair of hair as to be practically white, never without a cigarette between his lips, affected to take nothing (except snooker) seriously; Blair, silver-tongued and open-handed, was the Irishman's notion of an Irishman; Jackson was your archetypal Aussie – tall, laconic, lantern-jawed; Fardell, veteran of Burma, was quickly nicknamed 'Daddy', for his worried, kindly manner; Sanderson, a cool, urbane companion, had been so careless as to break his neck in a Middle East crash-landing, and wore a plastic collar that made his balding head look, from the back, like a boiled egg in a china cup; and Wright, whose persistent survival on a regimen of booze had flabbered Lanham's gast at Wickenby, now strode the tarmac in a uniform more raffish and a straggling moustache more RAFish than Tee Emm's cartoonist could conceive.

Sweeping in a long descent across the shiny ribbon of the Trent, I looked down on bomber country: Bottesford and Syerston, Balderton and Winthorpe, Swinderby and Waddington. Dead ahead, the great cathedral stood, towering over Lincoln, the seemingly eternal monument, the symbol of the future and the past, that I had put my faith in, when I had the need in 1943. It had stood upon the hill for centuries before the bombers came, and would stand there still, long after we were gone.

I knew then what had driven me to fly here – not to beat up Blyton, Wickenby or Sandtoft, although that would be fun – but to get my whammy going again, to touch the magic stone. Hey there, cathedral, look at me! I'm the guy who flew back home to you, night after night, remember? In the big, black beaut? Look at me now in my Mosquito, you great heap of masonry, and do your stuff. Keep my precious arse safe, when I take it over Germany again.

'Say hello to the old cathedral, Dicky, think nice thoughts about it – it'll bring us luck.'

'Wilco, skipper, but…'

'But what?'

'It's a funny feeling, looking up at a building – from an aeroplane.'

Flying south, and back at altitude, I started thinking of the crew again. The whammy was still looking after them, sometimes against the odds. Fairbairn's skin remained intact, although the aged Libs in which he flew could seldom reach the height they were supposed to. Protheroe was flying with fresh, green crews, with pilots who worried him more than those who flew the Messerschmitts. On one interesting operation, the mid-upper gunner had gone noisily insane; other members of the crew had dragged him from the turret and strapped him to the rest-bed while little George, extricated from the belly-guns, climbed up to take his place. Walker's Fortress, homeward bound, had flown into an anti-aircraft shell. Johnny, at a waist-gun, had woken up to find himself lying in the fuselage, and quite alone. Once before, he had flown a Lancaster, and an injured pilot, back to base, but he did not know so much about the front end of a Fortress, so he hit the silk. 'We thought,' his gallant crew-mates told him, when he rejoined them in some foreign field, 'that you were one dead Englishman.' He had proceeded to convince them he was not. Cassidy had gone to Dresden, in one of 1,400 heavy bombers, on the thirteenth of the month, to make a holocaust. A bigger fire than Hamburg, so they said, and, unlike Hamburg, undefended.

I had ambivalent emotions about that. The only city I had ever bombed that did not sturdily defend itself was Milan, and that was not because it could not – there were guns and lights in plenty, all working hard until the bombs began to fall – and it had been a weird experience to make the bombing run across a silent city, through static searchlights raised, like arms, in mute surrender. It was not that I liked being shot at – I hated it no end – but no more had I liked to bomb Milan that summer night. You would not bowl your fastest at a man who could not use a bat and, although I knew by now that war, and least of all the bomber war, was not a cricket match, I was glad that I had not had to go to Dresden.

'Alter course one-nine-five compass, please, skipper.'

'One-nine-five.'

I made the small correction with a touch of stick and rudder, and set the heading on the P4 compass. This aeroplane, the Mosquito Mark III, only needed touches to tell it what to do, but it really needed them. You did not sit back and let the Mossie fly itself for too long, as you could in every Halifax and many Lancasters. Go dreamy in this high-strung animal, and you might quickly find yourself, as many a line-book had been annotated, 'Upside-down, with nothing on the clock except the maker's name.' No airborne battleship or cruiser, the Mosquito: more of a frigate or corvette.

Never much inclined to engineering niceties, and even less so as I came to realise that aeroplanes could not care less how much or little you recalled about the workings of their inmost servos, pumps and valves, I judged an aeroplane a lot on how it looked, to what extent the cockpit met my physical requirements, and on how it smelt.

Like all good aeroplanes, the Mosquito looked as though it ought to fly well – the first glance told you that. There were those two, great, sharply-pointed engines slung below the tapered wings; the typically towering tail that said De Havilland's had made it; and the narrow fuselage, the famous mix of ply and balsa wood, which gave so high a ratio of power to weight.

Sitting in the cockpit was like eating at a crowded table – not a lot of room for knees and elbows. It would have been extremely cramped if you had needed lots of clothes, as in the freezing heavy bombers. Luckily, the cabin was as warm as toast, and I found that one issue polo-necked jersey underneath the battledress was quite enough for comfort.

Stretching the analogy of the dining-table further, you might also have felt that you were sitting at the very end, against the table-leg, so that you were slightly slantwise in your chair – not absolutely balanced fore and aft. At first, I thought that this sensation came because the blind-flying panel, the instruments on which you concentrated most, as would the diner on his plate, was not quite straight in front of you, but set a little to the right. In due course, however, another and more authoritative reason had been offered, by an instructor who was briefing some of us for night-flying.

'You will, by now,' he had said, 'be aware of "bottom effect" in the Mosquito.'

We had stared back at him blankly. Awareness was not immediately apparent in the group. Was this, I wondered, some aerodynamic phenomenon about the aircraft I had missed? Surely not, for I had promised Nina that I would not sleep a wink in Ground School, and I had kept my word.

'Of course,' the briefing officer had continued, 'the aircraft normally goes up and down through cloud too fast for it to bother you, but you will certainly have noticed it if you've been practising your IF properly.'

He had us there. To ask now for enlightenment would have been tantamount to a confession that peeking had been going on beneath the hood: that earth and sky, the pilot's friends, had not been totally obscured. And yet my conscience was as clear about the blind-flying canopy as it was about the Ground School. I stressed my senses under it as ardently as any medieval monk, in penance, had ever mortified his flesh. Surreptitiously, I had checked the faces of my colleagues. Jackson's features had been carved from hard, Australian wood; Fardell's expressed no more than the customary tired benevolence; Pearce's attention was entirely taken up with the delicate extraction of some extraneous matter from the depths of his left nostril; Blair's eyes were glazed, and I guessed his thoughts were more about the Banbury hotel room, where his newly-wedded wife was waiting, than with the present briefing. I might have felt the same, had Nina been that close. That was the trouble with a tendency to pottiness about a girl: your thoughts were always liable to stray.

'Go another five degrees port, skipper,' said Dixon. 'You should see Barford ahead in about three minutes.'

I pulled the rpm back to 1800, throttled the engines down to plus two pounds of boost, and changed to base frequency on the radio. The clipped, familiar chatter between the WAAF in the tower and pilots in the circuit whispered through my headphones as I began to pick up a pattern of landmarks that confirmed the navigator's forecast.

'D for Dog, approaching from the north,' I told the tower. 'Request permission to rejoin, over.'

'D – Dog, you're clear to rejoin. Runway two-four, QFE one-zero-zero-three, wind fifteen degrees from port, ten knots. Four aircraft in the circuit. Call downwind, over.'

The barometric pressure had fallen by one millibar since take-off, and that would make my altimeter over-read by thirty feet. It was an insignificant amount, in conditions of such visibility that you could trust your eyeball all the way, but I made the small adjustment to the datum out of habit, as part of the process of tidying up the cockpit for landing. This was no great exercise: the Mosquito, for all its power and capabilities, was a very simple aeroplane to manage. You could go straight into the circuit from the sky, and run through BUMPFF when you were downwind. The sequence did not quite conform to Pilot's Notes, but it had been imprinted on my memory for good, and it seemed to function just as well in the Mosquito as it had in any aircraft I had dropped on to a runway, anywhere. B for brakes – lever off and pressures adequate; U for undercarriage – selected down and two green lights to prove it; M was an anachronism –

Merlin engines took care of their own air-to-fuel mixtures –
but I kept to the mnemonic for old time's sake, and hoped it
would remind me to open the gills and shutters for cold air;
P for propellers – 2,850 rpm, and tighten up the friction nut
to stop the levers slipping back; F for flaps (down a little) and
fuel-cocks to main supply with boosters on. The Pilot's
Notes said 'Harness tight and locked', but I disliked the
straps, and only wore them if I meant to turn the aircraft
upside down, so that comprised the landing drill.

I kept the airspeed at 140 knots until the turn from base-
leg on to finals, and let it gradually decrease on the approach,
until the boundary fence passed underneath the nose at about
100, with the full flap down. Throttles chopped, stick back,
bubbling exhausts, the chequered pattern of the caravan
sliding past the edge of my left eyeball, and the Mosquito
dropped on to the runway like a stone.

At this point, with many aeroplanes – cheerful,
unsophisticated aeroplanes – there should be little more to
do. An occasional, relaxed swing of the rudder, in due course
a touch of brake, and you would be taxying back to your
dispersal, calm and collected, to scribble DCO in the
Authorisation Book – another detail carried out. But in the
Mosquito, you were not quite through with landing yet. Even
Pilot's Notes warned of a 'tendency to swing', and they were
compiled by men whose style inclined to understatement.
Knowing the language, I read that passage as 'Just watch it,
Jack, or your landing run will finish up in ever-decreasing
circles and a lot of broken balsa-wood,' and kept each nerve
a-twitter until all movement ceased.

Following this method, the first night-circuit's detail
passed without mishap. The sky at night had always been my
friend: I found it easier to concentrate on flying right in
darkness than I did amongst all the visual distractions of the
day. And, in the circuit, the clear-cut indications of the
airfield lighting – runway, peri-track and glide-path –
provided an environment that I knew well and trusted.

Whether Fardell or Blair felt that way, I did not know. If they did, their trust was cruelly misplaced. Trust, in fact did not have a good night. I had made my final landing shortly after 3 a.m., and, after egg and bacon in the Mess, cycled to the airmen's Nissen hut in which Barford St John was pleased to quarter commissioned aircrew under training. I had hardly closed my eyes, with the airfield lights still flickering behind them, when the door creaked open and the sound of careful footfalls broke the surface of the silence. Slightly surprised that any occupant was still out of his bed (I had had the circuit to myself for at least the last half-hour), but not particularly concerned, I was trying to push my face into the stiff, unfriendly pillow when a hand fell on my shoulder and a voice growled in my ear. 'Scuse me, sir.'

I turned my head. A corporal of the RAF Police was bending over me, and another stood beside him. Instinctively, I searched the pages of my conscience for a misdemeanour grave enough to bring these minions here, to hound me down in early dawn. 'Yes, Corporal,' I croaked, 'what is it?'

'Which is Flight Lieutenant Fardell's bed-space, sir, and…' He flashed a torch-light on his note-book. '…Flying Officer Blair's?'

The possibilities began to tumble through my mind. Perhaps my colleagues had been taken ill and, on landing, sent to hospital; or, for some reason, diverted to another airfield. The SPs had come to fetch their toothbrushes, and such… But, although I had never seen death's errands handled in this way before, I knew the truth before I asked the questions. 'Why, what's happened?'

'Flying accident, sir. Now, which…'

'How, where?'

'Don't know, sir. We have to collect the effects, see. Duty Officer's orders.'

The SPs were silent and efficient in their undertaking. When they had tiptoed from the hut, I rose and, pulling back the curtain, watched their van move off into the shadows taking with it every trace of Fardell and Blair: kitbags, cases, photographs on bedside-lockers, used towels and toilet-bags, everything.

No, not quite everything. On the floor between Fardell's bed and that of Sanderson (who slept serenely on) lay Fardell's favourite scarf, a green silk square, white-spotted – the scarf he always wore when he went flying. The silk slipped softly through my fingers as I folded it. That night, Fardell had flown without his whammy – not that it could have made a difference to his destiny. No more than the locker-key from Wickenby had made to mine, or the magic medallion that Jumbo Edwards had bequeathed, or Nina's nylon stocking in my pocket. Mascots, whammies, good-luck charms – all superstitious rubbish – I did not really credit it at all. That was what I told myself, for the umpteenth time, as I tucked Daddy Fardell's scarf into my kit-bag.

Someone in the hut began to snore, with mounting volume, until he woke himself, bit off the snore and slept again. Shivering, as the chill air crept through my pyjamas, I was starting to slide back between the blankets when I remembered that Blair, too, had left a part of him behind. Few knew about the waiting lady, in the Banbury hotel – his nightly visits there had never had official sanction – but now officialdom would have to know.

Outside, the stars were going into hiding from the coming dawn; even the three bright planets, that had moved along the southern skyline so boldly through the night, now seemed pale, in need of respite from their eternal, distant journey. I called the Duty Officer from the Guardroom – the nearest building, manned at that hour, with a telephone. Blair's crash, he said, had happened first. Then, ninety minutes later, Fardell's within a mile. Both pilots had been killed on impact. No, he did not know the cause of either. He would pass the information about Mrs Blair to Upper Heyford: 'They deal with all that sort of thing. I expect the Adj. will go and see her. I don't envy him that job.'

'The SPs came and cleared their kit out of the hut – they said you sent them.'

'Yes, that's the form.'

'Seemed a bit off, to me.'

'Don't quite follow you.'

'Like vultures. I mean, couldn't it have waited?'

'Unfortunately not, old boy. We used to find there was nothing left, once a fellow's chums knew he'd bought it. They were the vultures, actually! Next-of-kin were complaining, you know – Johnny's pocket-book and watch-chain gone – that sort of thing. Hard fact of life, old boy. So now we get in first.'

'I see.'

'I'd get back to the pit, if I were you. Night-flying again tonight, if the met's okay.'

Weaving in between the potholes and the puddles on the way, I mused upon the causes of the crashes. After all, experienced pilots like Fardell and Blair did not just fly into the ground without a reason. Engine failure was always the likeliest of explanations, but for that to happen twice to different aircraft in so short a time seemed to stretch coincidence too far; and the Merlin, furthermore, was seldom known to fail. Anyway, the wooden wonder, lightly-laden, uninhibited by drag from guns or long-range fuel tanks, should climb better on one engine than a Lancaster on three, although there had to be some careful balancing of power and rudder, and the speed had to be right. Mismanagement of the petrol system was another possibility. The drill was to use the contents of the outer wing-tanks first – which would not take long at circuit power – and then switch to the main supply, from the inner wing and centre-section; but the gauges for the outer tanks were about as reliable as railway timetables, and I supposed that, if you were used to tanks that fed into each other, and so forgot to turn the cock, or had a little bit of panic when one engine cut – or both – you might just find you had an aeroplane that would only fly downwards. And then there was that other strange phenomenon the briefing man had spoken of, which until now had slipped out of my mind.

My own instructor at Barford was one Flight Lieutenant Moody, a tall bony fellow with smoothly-waved, black hair and a face that you would notice in a crowd – strong cheek-bones, chin and nose. His battledress looked always newly cleaned and pressed, his shirt and collar straight out of the laundry. Add to this his pleasant voice and stylish manner, and you had the sort of chap who would have been a movie mogul's idea of a hot-shot pilot from a stately home – the sort of part that my old USAAC classmate Michael Rennie had so heroically essayed in one or two sub-epics of the early nineteen-forties.

It was this paragon whom I approached that evening, while Dixon got his gear together for a practice bombing detail. 'Forgive the expression,' I said, 'but what is "bottom effect"?'

I watched his eyes as he wondered whether, and decided not, to make a joke about it. 'In relation to the Mossie, you mean?'

I nodded.

'Who's been telling you about that?'

'I don't know, somebody mentioned it the other day. Said we ought to know about it, and I didn't.'

'You don't need to,' said Moody, shaking his glossy head and giving me the film-star smile. 'I'd have told you about it, if I thought you did.'

'Yes,' I persisted, 'but what is it?'

On the airfield, somebody pressed a Merlin's starter-button. That would be Pete Jackson, who was due first on the range. Moody leaned back against the crew-room wall and crossed one elegantly-trousered leg over the other. 'It's a sort of disorientation,' he said, patiently, 'that happens to people who won't believe their instruments. Your IF is good, you've done lots of it in the heavies, and you've kept in practice, so it won't affect you.'

I was pleased at that. No matter how many hours were in your log-book, a little praise from your instructor was always nice to hear. And flying by instruments, for me, had always been a chore: usually difficult, sometimes tedious, and never any fun. But the simple recognition of necessity, plus a powerful instinct for survival, had made me work at it. I knew you had to learn to trust, if not to love, that panelful of dials. And you had to learn to disregard conflicting indications that your so-called sense of balance gave you: those little sensors in your head were fine for standing up and sitting down, and turning corners without falling over, but they were worse than useless in the darkened cockpit of an aircraft. 'If God meant man to fly,' the cynics said, 'He would have given him a pair of wings.' He would also have equipped him with a more suitable device than those rather inefficient spirit-levels in the inner ear, which would do their utmost to convince you, when you straightened up after a long turn to the right on instruments, that you were turning sharply to the left; when levelling out from a steady climb, that you had gone into a dive; and vice versa, in both cases. If you believed their evidence, and tried to follow it, your blind-flying exercise would be interesting, but short.

'Aw, shucks,' I said, 'you're just saying that. I'd still like to know what bottom-effect is.'

'My dear chap, isn't it obvious? The rudder-pedals are slightly offset – you must have noticed that – so you're sitting with a bit more pressure on your left buttock than your right. That can make you think you're turning to port when you aren't. Now, do you mind letting me get on with my work – I haven't even started the *Telegraph* crossword today.'

On the climb, I briefly shut my eyes and tried to judge whether any feeling in my buttocks made me want to turn the aircraft madly to the right, but nothing happened. Not that that disproved the theory: except for taking-off and landing, or when badly frightened, I seldom sat up straight, but shifted around in the seat a lot, seeking the most comfortable position. Nevertheless, it was nice to have something to blame for sloppy flying.

'If I give you any shaky bombing runs, Dickie, just remember it's the dreaded bottom-effect I'm fighting against, okay?'

'Er – would you repeat, please, skipper?'

'Nothing, Dickie. Levelling out at fifteen thousand.'

Pete Jackson, we learned later, did not reach that altitude: at 10,000 feet, or thereabouts, there was a sudden, deafening silence from the Merlins. Following some earnest juggling with the fuel-cocks and boosters, which brought no response, he held a brief conference with Wiltshire, his fellow-Aussie navigator, and turned the rapidly-sinking aircraft back towards the lights of Barford. 'She glided like a bloody brick,' he subsequently stated. 'It didn't look like we were going to make it for a while there. The lower she got, the further a-bloody-way the airfield seemed to be. Old Wilt was saying his prayers, weren't you, cobber?'

'Too right. I was praying you wouldn't try and go round again when we got there, out of habit.'

'Pig's arse, habit,' said Jackson, automatically, and turned back to his small audience of pilots. 'I had a couple of goes at getting the fans turning, but no dice…'

'What speed did you use, Pete?' I asked.

'One-twenty, mostly – about five knots above the stall. Maybe I should've flown her faster, what d'you reckon?'

'Blowed if I know. It worked, anyway, didn't it?'

'Only bloody just, mate. Old Wilt pumped the wheels down, late as he dared, and we just scraped in over the fence. Ran out of brake-pressure, and finished up with a beaut ground-loop on the far side of the peri-track.'

He shrugged his shoulders, looking round the group with challenging, grey eyes, as though he thought that we might criticise his work. Wright slapped him on the back. 'Wizard show, Pete,' he said. 'A dead-stick landing from ten grand – absolutely wizard.'

We murmured our agreement, and the expression on Wiltshire's face was that of one navigator happy with his pilot.

I never heard why Jackson's engines failed, no more than I knew why Fardell and Blair had flown into the ground. Not that I made a point of seeking to find out: accidents and mishaps had occurred before, and would again. To probe their causes seemed indelicate, even morbid, in a man. To brood on death was unproductive – I had noticed that before. It could lead to drinking too much alcohol, and other patterns of irrational behaviour. By happenstance, I found such a case that very afternoon. PT was ordered for the course, which had to be avoided at all costs. I had so much practice in this line, starting with ardent fitness maniacs at ITW, on through the crew-cut calisthenicists of the US Army Air Corps and the muscle-bulging sadists of the glider units, that the fresh-faced PTI at Barford was as putty in my hands. 'Unfortunately, I'm not allowed PT,' I told him, 'not until the trouble with my spine clears up. Damn nuisance, but you know what they're like at CME.'

'CME, sir?'

'Central Medical Establishment. Wing Commander Thoroughgood – he's the spine specialist – he put me on swimming.'

The corporal frowned. 'We haven't got no baths here, sir. Not at Barford.'

'Really? In that case, it'll have to be the ten-mile walk.'

The token stroll I took along the quiet lanes was, initially, as therapeutic as Thoroughgood, had he existed, could have wished. Then I came upon the little boy – a pretty sight, kneeling at the roadside, his curly head bent over some plaything, which he was gently prodding with a stick, while crowing pleasantly with childish joy. As I approached, he stiffened, turning from his toy (which now revealed itself to be a small, furry animal, either comatose or dead), and fixed me with a malevolent, suspicious stare. I looked away, not wishing to intrude on the macabre entertainment, and strolled on as nonchalantly as you can when you know that little eyes are watching you. Coming abreast, and unable to resist another glance, I smiled benignly at the boy, receiving in exchange a glare of implacable hostility. Obviously, I had antagonised him in some way – perhaps there was a local ban on smiling on a Wednesday afternoon. I wiped the smile away, as though it had arrived upon my face by accident, and continued on my course.

As I walked, I took Nina's latest letter from my pocket, and read it through again. Why it had surprised me so was hard to say: perhaps it was that she had made her mind up, and taken action on her future, without reference to me. Certainly, her Flying Bomb Directorate would soon become redundant, with the eastward progress of the Allied Army Groups; but I had thought that she would stay in London, somewhere in the great maw of the Air Rouse, still living in her digs on Harrow Hill. But she had always hated the metropolis, and pined for open country, green fields and the flying scene. Once she knew that I was on Mosquitoes, she had figured I would find my way to 8 Group, and so had asked their Airships for a posting there herself. Within the week, she was at Warboys, Adjutant to Hamish MaHaddie, who trained the PFF navigators, in the flat, lush farmland north of Huntingdon. She was living in a Nissen hut, as I was, and loving it, as I was not. Five other women shared her quarters (that would have made all the difference, at Barford), 'two of them are bitches, one passable, the Flight Officer and the WAAF "G" are nice.' There were several Mosquito bases within reasonable distance – Wyton, in particular, was only three miles away. 'It would be wonderful if you could get a posting there.' Furthermore, she was in negotiation with one of the staff navigators for the purchase of his Morris Eight – good runner, only 80,000 miles on the clock, in need of taxing and insuring, but a bargain at £45 –

'then we can be together whenever you're on stand-down.' What a woman! I could see now why she, of all those radar girls, had been commissioned. I had, just because I was a pilot – she, because she was an organiser, born and bred. And she was organising me!

If I could have found another way back to camp, I would have taken it, but within half-an-hour or so, I was retracing my steps, and the troll-like child was once again in view. This time, small animals, extinct or not, appeared to be forgotten, and he presented a more human face – at least a face I knew – for he was engaged in foot-drill: marching, breaking into slow time, halting, turning about, marching off in quick time… 'That's the stuff,' I cried – determined to make some sort of contact, 'swing those arms, shoulders back, left-right, left-right, left!'

This approach had an even more bizarre effect than smiling on the boy. He dropped his poking-stick, which had been serving as a rifle for the purpose of his drill and, hurling himself through a gap in the hedge, disappeared across the fields and far away. I felt a little wounded by this, until I remembered that the well-established brooding syndrome was almost certainly to blame.

No good ever came of brooding – I knew that well enough myself. Inconsequential actions only, nothing positive or useful. Chaps who brooded seldom made decisions: when they did, they were inclined to be too late, and late decisions were only good for saying, 'I could have told you so.' You had to give that much to Nina – she was no brooder. I wondered, by one of those random, mental switches, whether she would have a baby soon. The anti-baby measures that we took – the 'precautions' – tended to be a little inconsistent. Pregnancy would see Nina out of uniform in no time flat, and then where would we be? 'Two can live as cheaply as one,' they said, and there was a bank manager in Harrow who could be relied upon to ensure we did just that, but what of three? I had made no sort of decision in this slightly crucial area; no more, I thought, had Nina, for all her organising powers. As for me, I had to face the fact that, unless you counted choosing which cereal to have at breakfast, or whether to fly through a cloud instead of round it, I was really not the big decision-maker I liked to think myself to be. It was not that brooding held me back; but that I seldom seemed to make my mind upon a course of action until the circumstances pointed at the only way to go. And at that very moment, back at Barford, circumstances were doing it again.

In the evening, I was working my way slowly through a half of bitter, when Pittam – one of the commissioned navigators – joined me at the hatchway in the corridor that served as a bar in Barford's mess. He was a burly, dark-haired fellow, maybe half an inch taller and a good stone heavier than I, and about my age, within a month or so. I knew that he had done a tour with 4 Group, on the Halifax, presumably starting as an NCO, like me, because he wore the ribbon of the DFM, and I had gathered that he showed an easy skill at high-speed navigation. I also knew he came from Lancashire, for which he could not be held to blame, and that he tended to be loud and boisterous when drinking beer – a less excusable defect.

'Cheer up,' he said, 'it might never happen.' He permitted himself a hearty laugh, and slapped a half-crown on the counter. 'Have the other half?'

'No, thanks.'

'Go on, have a bloody drink. Have a pint, then.'

'No, thanks. All right, I'll have a half.' Who said I was indecisive? It briefly crossed my mind to wonder why he sought to buy me beer, but I put the thought aside. Life was too short to look every gift horse – even one from Lancashire – directly in the mouth. And anyway, as Pittam talked, the picture cleared.

'They've scrubbed my bloke, did you know?'

'No, but I thought they might – he's pranged a couple, hasn't he?'

'Can't seem to keep straight on take-off. He's frightened me fartless, lots of times.' He laughed again, not quite so heartily.

'The Mossie does have a bit of a tendency to swing,' I said. 'I'm sorry he's been scrubbed.'

'Well, I am in a way. I mean, he's a decent enough bloke – just couldn't cope, that's all.' Half the contents of his glass vanished at a swallow. 'Did his first tour on Lancs.'

'So did I,' I said heavily, and moved aside, to give a thirsty-looking Jackson access to the bar.

Pittam followed me. 'Have you had much trouble on take-off yourself, then?'

I looked into his eyes – dark brown, serious, slightly bloodshot. Navigators did not usually concern themselves this way with pilots' little problems. 'My dear chap, don't be ridiculous,' I said, 'I'm an ace.'

He did not laugh. 'You're the only bloke to get above-average assessment on the course – I checked that.'

That was news to me, but I managed not to look surprised. 'Look, a swing's always waiting to happen – on take-off or on landing. I just try not to let it, that's all.'

He nodded, and took another swallow. That was half a pint destroyed in two shots. 'I'm going to have another one,' he said. 'What's the matter, don't you drink?'

'Yes, but this isn't a schooner race, is it?' I took his glass and had it refilled at the bar.

'Cheers,' he boomed. 'Extraordinary fortune.'

'Astonishing luck.'

'Where d'you reckon on going, then – after the course?'

'Leave.'

I had not meant to bring the house down, but he roared with laughter. Behind him, Jackson started nervously, and Wiltshire spilled a little beer. Pittam stopped laughing as suddenly as he had begun. 'After that, I mean.'

'I don't much mind. PFF would suit me – why?' He offered a cigarette. 'Ever heard of fourteen-oh-nine Flight?'

'No.'

He lowered his voice, bringing it down to the decibel-count of Aneurin Bevan addressing a public meeting. 'Met. reconnaissance. They're called the weather-spies.'

I remembered something Arthur Smith had said, a year ago, at Lulsgate – something about sending a Mosquito out before the heavies went. 'Oh, that,' I said. 'Sounds pretty boring to me.'

'Boring? It's bloody interesting,' he shouted. 'Blokes reckon it's the most interesting job in Bomber Command, these days.'

'What – checking the met. winds?'

'That's not all they do, for Christ's sake. Pre-attack target recce, photography, finding the fronts before they get to Europe… all sorts.'

I shrugged. 'It still sounds boring. But if that's your idea of fun – jolly good luck.'

He walked a step or two away, jingling the coins in his pocket. 'Apparently,' he said, 'they call for a new crew every four months.' He turned back, smiling, eyes bright with excitement. 'They want one now.'

Quick as ever on the uptake, I began to catch his drift. 'I see.'

'The thing is, the crew have got to be above average, and they've got to be officers.'

'Well, that lets me out – I'm crewed with Dixon.'

'Sure,' he said. 'But there could be a switch – if you're game.'

A WAAF orderly brushed past us, short and squat, thick-ankled, with a mask of brownish powder on her face. Pittam leered at her. 'Hello, beautiful,' he crooned. She frowned demurely, and reached up to fix the blackout curtain in an exercise that focused his attention on the movement of her heavy bosom.

'Where,' I asked him, 'is this Met. Flight, anyway?'

'Eh? Oh, it's near Huntingdon – place called Wyton.'

The gliders flew out on the 24th of March. High over Oxfordshire, I watched part of the procession pass below, slow, deliberate and clumsy, on course for the Rhine. Alf Gittins, I thought, would be down there, in the creaking cockpit of a Horsa – he and Archbold, and all those eager youngsters. But for the coupled hands of fate and an ever-loving mother, I would have been there with them in that aerial traffic-jam, not secure and snug in the Mosquito. Envy and relief competed in my conscience to be recognised as truth – relief came in an easy first.

8

Met Flight to Victory

The westward sky was full of thunderclouds, a line of ghostly battlements above the German coast. The anvil-top ahead of me was brilliantly white – whiter than a prince's pillow-case, or Caribbean teeth, or angels' wings. Pittam and I were flying at 25,000 feet, and it hung above us, dazzling in the April sun. Underneath that flattened head, in the great mass of the cloud, were thousands of gallons of water, in vapour, rain and hail; profligate discharges of electricity spasmodically occurred, each enough to light a city for a week. There was ice in there, and airframe-breaking turbulence. That cloud was trouble, from the bottom – which was pouring rain on Emden – to the top. Its name was cumulo-nimbus, and people back in Huntingdon, at PFF Headquarters, would be interested to know that it was there.

Pittam plotted the position in his log, and took a photograph through the front perspex with the hand-held camera. 'It's a big bugger,' he observed. 'Are you going through it?'

I nodded, grimly. It was the moment I knew must come, like the moment when you faced the bully who, last time you met, pushed you in the ditch and threw your cap away. If I had been alone in the Mosquito, I might have tried to dodge the brute, or climb above it; but with Pittam there – well, I simply nodded, grimly, and remained on course. Anyway, once you started weaving in and out of thunderclouds, you were liable to end up going round in circles in the middle of the biggest one.

I pulled the throttles back a little, settling the speed on what the bible said was right for turbulent conditions – 230 knots –and sat up straight, feeling the tension of the harness-straps against my thighs and shoulders. The great, white shroud came closer. Now there was no blue above, no brown or green beneath. I fixed my eyes upon the instruments, told myself to trust them, tried to keep my hands and feet relaxed, my breathing slow. Pittam sat beside me, utterly forgotten. In clouds, there were no colours, no more than in dreams – just different shades of grey. It gave you the sensation that you lacked reality, that if you pinched yourself you could awaken to the well-known, coloured world. And yet, by paradox, it was the clouds, the mists, the ice and every sort of weather, that made the true experience of flying in the war. All the other nastiness was fantasy; the sudden streams of incandescent bullets, the twinkling bursts of flak, the great, red pools of fire in unknown cities far below – they were the stuff to make a nightmare from.

Now that I was in the cloud, I ceased to be afraid. My task had been defined by circumstance, and it was very simple. All I had to do was to fly this aircraft straight and level for a while. If I could not do that, I did not deserve to wear the wings upon my chest: Wallace Bacon Sheffield and Lieutenant Sena would not care to say that they had taught me, and I could never call myself an ace again, not even as a joke.

What happened next was total anti-climax. There was no frightful, electro-magnetic flash, no bang, no sudden film of ice accreting on the wings, no stomach-wrenching turbulence; only the Merlins' steady hum, and the whisper of the airstream, as we passed without a tremor through the summit of the cloud, like a comb passed by a barber through a sleeping giant's hair. It was as though you had steeled yourself to go in against Larwood on a bumpy pitch, and he had bowled you lobs. Later, I reasoned that the thunder-cloud was dying, that the up-currents no longer reached its head, and that the icy particles were old, too cold and dry to cling to the Mosquito's skin. Huntingdon would want to know about that, too.

West of the front, the sky was clear, except for a broken layer of fluffy strato-cumulus, 20,000 feet below, through which occasional glimpses of grey-green suggested that the North Sea was still where it had always been. Behind us, two long streams of vapour trailed, as though forgotten kettles continuously boiled within the Merlins, making perfect guide lines for an interceptor – had any been around to notice in that piece of sky. Fortunately, the Luftwaffe only had one type of aircraft that could catch the Mossie, and the few they had of those were far away back east. The fact was that the jet-powered Me 262, which Professor Messerschmitt had planned before the war began, had been greeted by the German High Command with much the same white heat of apathy as their British counterparts had shown for Whittle's baby. Like the Meteor, the Me 262 had been an unwanted and neglected child. That well-known aviation expert, Adolf Hitler, had not liked it from the start, which, in the first years of the war, gave it as much chance of promotion as I had of becoming Chief of Air Staff. Not that anybody in the higher reaches really pressed its cause: it was as though the great Air Marshals, on both sides of the Channel, did not want the boys to play with toys that they themselves had never known. When, at last, a few were built for use as fighters, they made a startling impact. On 7th April 1945, they got amongst the Mustang escort of a daylight mission and shot down 28. Everyone was rather worried for three days, then 1,200 heavies made a point of visiting their bases near Berlin, and virtually put them out of business. They were withdrawn to the area of Prague, and never really threatened anyone again.

In fact, at this stage of the war, any threat to the Mosquito was unlikely to be from action by the enemy. It existed either in the weather, in the aeroplane itself, or in some failure by the crew to fly it right. An essential element of flying on ops was missing, and it bothered me. There was nothing to be scared of any more – no Focke-Wulfes or 109s, no skylines full of flak and searchlights. If I was ever frightened now it had to be of weather or the Mossie – or myself. Or any combination of those three.

'Two-five-oh should get us back to base,' said Pittam, 'or near enough.'

He never asked, as other navigators did, for 249 or 251 degrees, or maybe 248 or 252, according to their calculations. He seemed to know that it was easier to steer along a main division of the compass – on five or zero – so he picked the nearest, and made up for it later with a right or left correction. An easy man to live with in the air was Norman Pittam; and, on the ground, we had established a tolerable *modus vivendi*, if not to say rapport. At Wyton, this had really been essential, because most members of the Weather Flight lived in a biggish, pre-war OMQ, with each room housing one aircrew. Pittam and I enjoyed a bedroom where, as I imagined, some Flight Lieutenant of the 1930s had kissed his youngest child goodnight.

So closely juxtaposed, we soon knew all about each other – all that we had not found out before, at Barford. I had felt some guilt in jettisoning Dixon, but he had met the situation with a stolid equanimity which, though it relieved my conscience, was not entirely flattering. 'Of course, you want to be near your wife, sir,' (he had reverted to immediate formality on the break), 'I'd be the same.'

'I didn't know you were married, Dicky.'

'I'm not – not yet. But if I was, I'd do the same as you.'

In fact, for several months I was to spend more time in Pittam's company, by day and night, than ever in my wife's. And, when I had the chance to visit her, he – like the girlfriend's mother of whom Jack Buchanan sang – came too. Luckily, Nina took a liking to him from the start, treating him as though he were a favourite, if naughty, younger brother, to be kept, with all affection, in his place. She soon discovered that a determined tickling beneath the lower ribs reduced him to a helpless, shrieking jelly, and so had little difficulty in keeping order. The merest threat of this corrective became enough to send him into panic flight, wild-eyed and bellowing 'No, Nina, please! No!' With other exits barred, on one occasion in the WAAF OQ at Warboys, he somehow scrambled through a casement window, headlong into the outer darkness, leaving shreds of skin, of battledress, and the echo of an anguished cry behind.

Comfortably seated, toying smugly with a mug of cocoa, I took a lot of pleasure in the scene. It brought back memories of the escape drills at Barford, when we had practised leaving the Mosquito in a hurry. Pittam had to go out of the tiny nose-hatch first – not for any altruistic thought of mine that, as the captain, I should be the last to leave – but for the better reason that, if he did not clear the way, I could not go at all. My part was to follow closely, but not so closely as a strong survival instinct, on our early efforts, drove me to. The ensuing all-in wrestling matches took so long to settle that the parachute instructor had been moved to irony. 'Four minutes, twenty-five seconds,' he observed. 'If that's the best you can do, gentlemen, I shouldn't bother. Just sit back and say the Lord's Prayer.'

There were mutual recriminations. 'It beats me how you ever passed for aircrew, Pip,' I told him. 'Your reactions are so bloody slow.'

'Balls. It's you panicking that's the trouble. You nearly did me a serious injury.'

'All you've got to do is get out of the way, you turgid great oaf.'

'How can I, with your bloody legs round my neck?'

It took a lot of bruising, sweating practice before we got our act together, but at last we clicked: Pittam slid out of his seat like a performing seal, hit the mattress on the hangar floor, and rolled aside as I flopped down beside him. The instructor pressed the button of his stop-watch. 'Sixty-two seconds. That's more like it. All you've got to do now is deploy your parachutes – you do remember how to do that, don't you, gentlemen? Right, let's try it just once more, shall we? I mean, my old grannie could beat sixty seconds, and she's got rheumatoid arthritis. And this time perhaps you'd like to practise stopping the starboard engine before you jump. I mean, we don't want you coming down with some vital parts missing, do we?'

Then, because the Mossie flew so high, the aircrew had to pass more tests. There was an ordeal by vacuum, in the decompression chamber, from which the atmosphere was gradually withdrawn and then put back, while you sat there twiddling your thumbs and hoping that you would not get the bends. The oxygen test was undertaken in another metal cylinder, where you and seven fellow-sufferers sat face-to-face in rows of four, listening to dictation through your headphones and trying to write it down, while the white-coated torturers outside imperceptibly reduced your vital life-support resource.

There were variations between one man's resistance to anoxia and another's, but not a lot. Everybody's script became in turn a scrawl, a shaky line across the page and, finally, a blank. When they pumped the air back in, you began to write again, like a toy whose clockwork was rewound, and no one had the slightest memory of the lacuna in their lives. This was no surprise, for I recalled how Lanham gabbled nonsense from his turret, the night a little chunk of flak had cut his oxygen supply at 20,000 feet above the Ruhr. He, too, had regained his senses when I took the Lancaster below 10,000 feet, and had boggled at us when we told him what he had said.

The medical officer who had charge of the proceedings, brisk and bright, admonished us. 'All you people could do a lot to improve your tolerance, you know. And your general state of health.'

We stared at him woodenly, sensing he would tell us something horrid. He did. 'Cut out cigarettes and alcohol – it's as simple as that.'

Tony Wright gasped, like an innocent defendant

sentenced to the cat. 'Steady on, Doc! It's only booze and fags that keep me going.'

With a practised glance, the MO took in the tall, round-shouldered figure in the crumpled battledress, the incipient pot-belly, the drooping, tobacco-stained moustache, the putty-coloured cheeks and baggy eyes, beneath the frayed peak of a battered SD cap. He smiled.

'What I'm suggesting is,' he said, 'that you'd probably keep going a lot longer without them.'

'Wouldn't be worth it, Doc,' said Wiltshire, with that certainty of statement all Australians acquire as soon as they can talk. 'That's all we poor bastards have to live for – that and sheilas.'

The practised eyes were turned on him, and then upon the rest of us, seeing yet more pallid skin, more lax deportment, more evidence of dissipation. I thought it was a pity that Paddy Blair was not still with us, for he had been a fine, upstanding, healthy-looking man. Even Daddy Fardell would have improved our corporate appearance – at least his whiskers had not looked like rotting hay, nor his eyes like poached eggs on a plate.

The MO pursed his lips, closed his small, black bag, and left us to our wretched destiny.

As it happened, destiny (in one of those moves upon the chequerboard of life described by old Khayyam as playful) had sent, not only Wilt and Jackson, but Tony Wright to one of Wyton's squadrons a week before Pittam and I arrived to join the Met. Flight, and one of our first impressions of the place, as we sat sipping a midday shandy in the empty bar-room, which was located in the spacious entrance-hall, had been provided by my old 12 Squadron colleague's sudden ingress. Moving briskly, fumbling for coinage in his pocket, he had tripped and, fighting a running battle with the force of gravity across the full length of the hall, had come to rest across the bar with his chin upon the counter. Unmoved, the barman had regarded him enquiringly. 'Yes, sir?'

'No need to break a leg, Tony,' I had advised him, 'the bar won't close for an hour or more.'

Pittam had expressed enjoyment of the action with a fruity roar of laughter, and Wright had tilted his head in our direction. 'Oh, hello, you fellows. Must have caught me foot in the bally carpet. D'you care for a snort?'

With his chin still on the counter, he had tipped the beer into his mouth in the way he used to do at Wickenby, so that his shaking hand would spill no drop. Did destiny intend, I wondered, to hold this abominable example in front of me throughout my second tour, as it had throughout my first? Would Lanham's prophecy be nightly mocked at Wyton, as at Wickenby?

Having swallowed half the contents of his glass, Wright had stood up straight and glowered at what was left. 'I'll beat you yet, you bastard,' he had muttered. 'Sure you won't join me, you fellows?'

We had still declined, although I knew that, in a literal sense, it was safe to join him, once he had digested his first pint. Until then, so noxious was his wind that only those who did not know him ventured near. Furthermore, in the crew-rooms of Wickenby it had been common knowledge that, when in the air, his dreadful vapours would break out again, so powerfully that those who shared a cabin with him could not survive unless they used their oxygen from take-off. And that had happened in the spacious Lancaster: in the confines of the Mossie's cockpit, I feared greatly for his navigator's health.

In his cheerful scruffiness, Wright did not stand quite alone at Wyton, but he was rather the exception than the rule. The 8 Group crews had been encouraged to regard themselves as a corps d'élite, and most of them made an attempt to look the part. The wealth of smoothly-barbered hair, of neat moustaches, cool, clear eyes and well-pressed battle-dresses made a striking contrast with the more *outré* appearance of the main force men at Wickenby. There were no Stetson hats or cowboy boots at Wyton; nobody wore Irving coats or sweaters in the splendid Mess. For once, it was the officers of other trades – administrators, engineers and flying controllers – who seemed, comparatively, less sartorially aware. Of a chaplain, and one of the doctors, down-at-heel and out-at-elbow, this was particularly true.

Even among such image-conscious fliers, the Met. Flight crews were noticeably elegant and couth. Most elegant and couthest of their number was our Squadron Leader, whose style and manner would have made the blessed Partington, at Upper Heyford, feel at home. He reminded me of everybody's favourite prefect at John Lyon's School – manly in a sort of boyish way, gently firm, dedicated to a strong belief in the joys of teamwork, always bound to do the decent thing, in the unshakeable conviction that one's chaps would follow one's example and, therefore, do it too. To see the Squadron Leader stroll into the Met. Flight hangar, from a four-hour Pampa to the Baltic ports and back, was to see again the popular prefect return to the pavilion after yet another chanceless, graceful innings for the school.

It was not his fault that my inward eye saw other Squadron Leaders, trudging into the debriefing room at Wickenby, blank-eyed, dishevelled, struggling to stay awake. No happy, pink-cheeked navigator trotted briskly after them, but pallid gunners in their heavy, heated suits; freezing bomb-aimers, stiff flight-engineers; and the navigators, blinking in the naked light, lugging canvas bags and sextants. All men, indeed, who had been there and back (as Docherty observed at Shobdon), had not enjoyed it very much, and wanted nothing more to do than go to bed. The Weather Flight Commander and his navigator – who doubled, incidentally, as his Adjutant – were, by contrast, now ready for a day's work at their desks.

This was indeed another war they waged at Wyton, as different from Wickenby's as rounders was from cricket. Not so much for the LNSF Squadrons, 128 and 163 – that was a difference mainly due to the height and speed of the Mosquito – but for the Weather Flight it really was a difference, both in intention and result. We carried neither bombs nor armament, but long-range fuel-tanks and cameras. No circling for height above the base for us, no zigzag route to dodge the hot spots on the way, no bomber stream to stay with for the safety of its numbers – just take-off, climb en route, straight to where you had to go; down the sky and up again to check the cloud base, the temperature and humidity (that was called a Thum), take shots of any interesting phenomena and back to base, like a boomerang, to tell the story on the scrambler telephone to the HQ weathermen.

The ambience of the unit was very like that of the highly self-regarded 'D' Instructors' Flight at Sandtoft, although, being operational, its members had rather more excuse for being so overtly happy with themselves.

There were ten crews in the Flight, all specially selected, and to carry out our special tasks we had six special aeroplanes – Mark XVIs in PR blue with pressure cabins – plus one unspecial, and unpressurised, Mark IX.

I had no doubt the ground crews, too, were specially selected. They were certainly efficient, and mechanical-type snags were rare. I had just one at Wyton – that was with an overheating engine, on a late night pre-attack reconnaissance. Halfway up the climb, at 15,000 feet or so above the sea, the port oil-pressure gauge dropped way below the minimum of 45 pounds per square inch, while the oil and coolant temperatures began to rise a little faster than the aeroplane itself. Opening the shutters made no difference, so I feathered the propeller, cut the petrol and ignition, in accordance with the drill. At this, the aeroplane declined to go on climbing. In fact, it would not hold the altitude it had. It could not be held to blame for this recalcitrant behaviour: not only were all internal tanks bung-full of petrol but it carried more in so-called drop tanks underneath each wing. These, you were supposed to jettison if an engine failed, but it had been found (and quickly passed along the pilots' grapevine) that, when you pressed the button, one tank would sometimes fail to fall away. By that law – 'Sod's Law' – which ordains you always drop your slice of toast marmalade-side down, the tank that did not drop would be on the same side as your sick engine, and so give your aeroplane the flying characteristics of a one-winged pregnant duck. Even as it was, with everything in place, you had to take care with the landing – fly the circuit high and at 145 knots (plus one or two for mother's sake), leave half-a-minute for the wheels to come down, because you only had half hydraulic power, and, since the port engine's air compressor was the one that charged the brakes, make sure there was a lot of runway there to play with.

If anything was more shame-making than being towed – backwards – into our dispersal by a tractor, it was having Pittam's flight-plan snatched away and handed to the crew, who had been called from bed to sit, with engines running, in the reserve aircraft, ready and eager to succeed where we had so conspicuously failed. Conspicuously, for no matter at what hour you made a single-engined landing (not for practice – nobody cared about that – but because you had to), you were certain of an interested audience. The balcony of flying control, high hangar windows, and any other vantage point, would invariably be full of conscientious ghouls. They might be men who did not even know you, nor you them, but they all had their own reasons for being there the night you broke your neck.

It seemed bad form to disappoint them. Bad enough to come back early, with the mission uncompleted: the least a chap could do was to provide an interesting conclusion. I had almost done that once – the only time the Lancaster had failed me. With both port engines gone, I had turned away from Stuttgart to crawl back, crab-wise, to the coast of Kent, to overshoot the nearest runway twice, and only to survive and try again because there was a dip beyond. West Malling's night-fighter crews, led by their commander 'Cats-eyes' Cunningham, had of course turned out to watch the fun. But there we had been something of a novelty – the seven, disappointed, slightly shaken men, the battered Lancaster among the sleek Mosquitoes; there, the bar had been re-opened and Cunningham himself had poured the beer. At Wyton, Pittam and I slunk silently away to baby's bedroom.

Meanwhile, in Europe, Eisenhower's armies were pressing on regardless, deep into the centre of Western Germany, and the Russians were advancing just as quickly from the east. At a proper squadron briefing, I would have seen the lines drawn on the map that showed where everybody was, but in the Weather Flight we were supposed to brief ourselves, and a hasty glance at the front page of whatever newspaper was left lying in the ante-room did not always print the latest battle-lines upon my mind. Unaware, therefore, that General Montgomery, in his wisdom, had seen fit to let the 2nd Army bypass most of Holland on their eastward march, I was cruising nonchalantly along the Dutch coast at about 8,000 feet, while Pittam took his photographs, when suddenly the sky around us was full of patent breaches of the peace.

'Pip,' I said, 'can you see a Jerry kite behind us?'

He put down the camera, and craned his neck. 'All clear.'

'That's funny – those gunners are firing at something.'

More bursts appeared in front of us, like balls of dirty cotton-wool. I changed course, hastily. Pittam's eyes were wide, above the mask. 'You're right,' he said, 'they're firing at us!'

'Bloody gunners,' I complained. 'Don't they know a Mossie when they see one?'

'Course they do – they're Jerry gunners. The buggers must still have got this bit of coast.'

I felt, not only shocked, but personally affronted. People were not supposed to offer the Mosquito violence. This was a case of unexampled cheek. It was also, I remembered, positively dangerous. Immediate departure from the scene, however ignominious, recommended itself. I commenced a steeply diving turn towards the sea, and pushed the throttles forward through the gate. 'Come on, D–Dog,' I urged, 'you're supposed to be the fastest piston-engined warplane in the world – now's the time to prove it.' The needle of the ASI moved past 400 knots, and the fragile airframe trembled. 'I wonder what speed the wings would come off at?'

'The way you're going,' growled Pittam, 'we'll soon find out.'

A long, low strip of land appeared ahead, with the dazzle of the sea on either side. I brought the engines back to cruising power and levelled out. The trembling subsided – the airframe's, anyway. I tried to read the folded map on Pittam's lap. 'Are the Jerries on the Frisians still?'

'I wouldn't be surprised.'

'You ought to mark it on the chart. In colour. Green for friend and red for foe, or something.'

'Oh, sure. What about little swastikas and Union Jacks?'

'Then we might not keep flying over flak batteries at 8,000 bloody feet.'

'They didn't hit us.'

The sinister, dark strip was coming quickly nearer. 'That island at twelve o'clock,' I said, 'it wouldn't be Texel, would it? Or Terschelling?'

'How do I know? If you get the props out of the water and climb a bit, I'll take a Gee fix.'

'They used to have some pretty nasty guns there, in the old days.'

'I know they did.'

'Well, then…'

I made a dog-leg round the island, just in case. I had been wrong about the fright going out of flying.– it was still around, if you went looking for it. I remembered Protheroe's remark that 'ops are a piece of piss these days, but some poor sods still seem to get the chop.'

I took the Mossie up to altitude and back to finish with the bit of weather we had been sent to look at. Flying home into the blinding spotlight of the setting sun, I revealed my thought to Pittam. 'Nina would be pretty cheesed off if I got the chop, you know.'

'Can't think why,' he said, pencilling the weather-readings in his log.

'Would anybody care if you did?'

'Did what?'

'Got the chop?'

He looked up, shading his eyes with his writing hand. 'One or two totties might.' He bent his head again, and wrote another line. 'And my mum and dad.'

'Well, then...'

We landed in the early evening and, when Pittam had phoned the weather story through to Huntingdon, we drove back in the Hillman flight van to our quarters for a wash and change of collar. We had a plan to pick up Nina from the Waafery at Warboys and, together, sup a couple in the village pub. That was the plan – the mechanics of the venture were against us. The Morris Eight stood, off-black and angular, behind the Mess. Its battery was flat, its tyres threadbare, its tank as innocent of petrol as the cupboard at the Hubbards' place of bones. We could crank the engine, we could take our chances with the tyres, but the lack of fuel really was a problem.

Thoughtfully, I kicked the offside front wheel. A few flakes of paint fell tiredly from the mudguard. 'Let's take the Hillman,' I suggested. 'Nobody'll need it tonight.'

'Misuse of Service transport,' said Pittam, sententiously. 'You're not supposed to take it off the Station.'

'There are lots of things you're not supposed to do. So what?'

'So we're not going to sit up and beg to be court-martialled. Even you aren't that bloody silly.'

'God, you're boring.' I kicked the tyre again. A brief

shower of rust fell on my foot.

Pittam sauntered round the car and stood beside me. 'What we could do,' he murmured, 'without anyone being any the wiser...'

'Yes, yes, yes?'

'We could siphon some juice out of it.' He stuck his thumbs under his armpits, grinning, wiggling his fingers and pushing out his chest, every inch the man to send for when you had a problem.

'Siphon? All I know about siphons is to do with soda.'

'Talk about me being boring – you're bloody useless. All we need is a bit of rubber tube and a good suck. I'll show you.'

While he was showing me, both of us crouched between the Morris and the van, I became aware that we were not alone. Our Squadron Leader, as dapper and serene as ever had come among us, the happy prefect on his nightly round. 'Hello, chaps,' he drawled. 'Trip all right this afternoon?' A tiny frown formed on his forehead. 'I say Pittam, old boy – what on earth are you up to?'

Pittam did something dextrous with the tube and stood erect, delicately spitting petrol to one side. He was wearing the commissioned NCO expression, full of rugged honesty, that came to him when at his most deceptive. 'Van tank's dry, Sir, I'm siphoning some of Currie's juice in, to get it operational.'

The prefect was impressed. He categorised our action as a jolly good show, in the best tradition of Weather Flight behaviour. But he was sure old Currie needed his petrol just as much as 8 Group did, and Pittam was at once to put it back in old Currie's tank. He, meanwhile, would instruct the duty MT chappie to come round with a can. He wished us both a very good night, and looked forward to seeing us, bright-eyed and bushy-tailed, in the morning.

We chorused a dutiful response, and Pittam, returning to his task, was so afflicted by a suppressed fit of the giggles that he swallowed half a mouthful of the petrol. He said, and later put it to the test, that it would take three pints of beer at least to get rid of the taste.

While we spied on the weather, and did silly things like this between our flights, the soldiers, grinding on towards the Elbe, were fighting their war in the way Sir Mike had said they must to win – with both feet on the enemy's terrain. The wheel had turned: from Dunkirk through to D-Day, it had been the bombers' war in Europe – no other arm could touch the German in his Fatherland. But now it was the soldiers' turn to beat the drum, and Bomber Harris danced to Eisenhower's tune.

On their march, the soldiers met with horrors which, at 30,000 feet, we never knew. Recently, a British Guards detachment had moved into a place that truly merited the description 'hell on earth'. The Guards found 40,000 living souls at Belsen: living, but with many on the point of death, from long, deliberate starvation. Tens of thousands more had died. Some lay in heaps about the camp, others in open pits, while Mother Nature tidied up in her slow, quiet way. These, in an area intended by its careful architects to accommodate 8,000. It stood now as a monument to Adolf Hitler and that fine body of men, the SS Corps, who were its warders. And it was only one of many such.

'Honestly,' said Nina, 'it really makes you wonder about the human race. And I don't just mean the men – some of the most awful brutes there were women.'

I was glad the Guards had found the camp at Belsen: it was what I needed. I had felt for months that I was moving on a given course, not from any impetus, but by inertia, like a body in a vacuum. If Belsen and its tortured tens of thousands did not provide the impetus, then nothing would.

'When we've beaten Germany,' said Nina, seeming to switch the subject, and yet following my thoughts, in the uncannily intuitive way that could persuade me I had spoken them aloud, 'will you and Pip have to go to the Far East?'

Pittam spluttered into his glass. 'I wish you wouldn't say

things like that – specially when I'm drinking.'

'Let's not worry about that,' I said, 'until the time comes. Let's see us in Berlin first.'

'The Russians are going to beat us there,' said Pittam. 'They're only thirty-five miles away – at least, they were this morning. They're probably closer than that by now.'

I stared at him. 'I can't make you out, Pip. You know exactly where the Red Army is, from hour to hour, but you haven't a clue about our own chaps' lines. There's something pretty sinister about that.'

It was fun to bring him to the point of saying a naughty word, even to uttering the opening explosive consonant, before the threat of Nina's active disapproval came into his mind.

'Bal... whoops! I mean, er, bally good grog, isn't it?' He stood up, averting his eyes from Nina's pursed lips and the fingers gently tapping on the trestle table. 'I'll get more, shall I?'

'Not for me, thank you, Pip,' said Nina, in her best WAAF-officer voice, which took her out of the mezzo-soprano register down to a full contralto, 'I've never really seen the fun in sloshing down drink all evening until it runs out of your ears.'

'It's not his ears it runs out of,' I said. 'I'll only have a half, Pip, and I hope you'll do the same. I'd rather not have you waking me up all night. staggering out to the loo.'

Pittam paused. 'I don't stagger – I move like a well-oiled machine.'

'Well-oiled is right.'

'At least I don't do it in the bed, like some I could mention.'

Nina's reaction was ambivalent. 'Pip, you are disgusting... who does that?'

'I'm not sure I ought to tell you.' He turned his head away in feigned embarrassment.

'Oh, go on. Not Jack?'

'Apart from Jack.'

'Well, who?'

'Our Groupy – the jolly old Station Commander.'

She gave a peal of disbelieving laughter. 'What nonsense! How could you possibly know that?'

'His batman told ours, and he told me. Wets the bed every night, regular as clockwork.'

'Pip! You're making it up!'

'Honour bright, Nina.'

'Poor man…'

'The batman? I should say so. Has to change the bedclothes and the mattress every morning.'

'I mean the Group Captain – the poor fellow must be ill.'

'I'm beginning to feel rather ill, myself,' I said. 'Are you going to buy some beer, or aren't you?'

I had heard that tale about the Group Captain, and found it weird and wonderful, like one of Grimm's about the strange ways of the fairy folk. I had carefully observed the man, as he stood smiling in his corner of the bar at lunchtimes, and wondered what it was that had afflicted him with such a weakness. He was bulky and broad-shouldered, with a pleasant face, round-cheeked but pale – too pale. Between his wings and the eagle PFF badge were ribbons of the DSO and DFC, with bars on both. He seemed very young to hold so high a rank, but so did many more in PFF's élite ranks. Again like several more, he was at times affected by a minor facial twitch. His youthfulness I found a little disconcerting – raised on such Group Captains as Crummy and Eric Nelson I looked for men of a slightly more paternal age and sort – the tic was less remarkable, for his position did seem to involve a little stress. Not only did he have to run the airfield, with two squadrons and the Met. Flight, but he also had the Group Commander, Donald Bennett, breathing down his neck, and living in the residence – the CO's quarters – which was rightly his. And Bennett, navigation ace and mastermind of target-marking tricks, was a man who tirelessly insisted on nothing other than the best. Another factor was that Wyton, being the nearest bomber base (of any comfort) to the capital, attracted VIPs like a bedside lamp did moths. Winston Churchill came with Eden, saw the squadrons go, had dinner in the Mess and settled in the ante-room, cigar and brandy-glass in hand, with the 8 Group high and mighty clustered round to cherish every word. It was the first time I had seen him since the 1940 Harrow Speech Day, and there was a noticeable difference in the man.

The puckish look, the cherub cheeks and twinkling eyes that I remembered were not now there to see; instead, a still solidity, an almost sullen, brooding strength. Though stout and sturdy in physique, he was not a big man; sitting there, however, in his black, House of Commons suit, chin sunk in chest, where waistcoat-buttons strained, he had a massive presence. His eyes had no more spark than coals that had been banked down for the night, although you felt that – with a fresh draught in the morning – they would glow again. An English gentleman, you would have said, certainly of grandpa vintage, quite well-to-do, who had enjoyed a lot of action in his time, and might not quite be done with action yet.

The lower orders (which, for that night's exercise, meant Squadron Leaders and below) soon went their ways, leaving the ante-room to the old hero and his multi-ringed, beribboned entourage. Pittam and I took beer into the billiards-room, and made a four with two more from the Met. Flight. Both tables were in constant use, and the seats along the panelled walls soon filled with people waiting for their turn. Waiters from the bar moved in and out with loaded trays. 'Oh, good shot,' someone called, and I saw that Eden, lolling in a window-seat, was following the game. What if the great man, I wondered, should cast round for his shadow in the ante-room, and find it gone, perhaps cut off, as Peter Pan had feared? The shadow, clearly, did not care. 'Jolly good shot,' he said, and lifted Scotch and soda to his lips. The handsome face was gaunt, the face of an exhausted man and, when next I looked, the whisky glass was cradled in his lap, his head lay back against the blackout curtain, and his eyes were closed.

Then the Russian party came – a dozen of them – squat, high-cheek-boned men with narrow eyes and non-existent hair. At Bennett's whim, our Group Captain had a firework display laid on by the armourers on the front lawn of the Mess. Route-marker flares and target indicators of all colours were ignited on the grass while the visitors, grouped on the steps, watched, if not inscrutably, without much evidence of scrute. The Mess gardeners' views about the show, it was reported, were more impassioned.

Visiting the cloakroom, I peeped inside one of the peaked, Red Air Force caps which hung upon the pegs, and found that Alkits had provided it. It was as though Attila's boot had borne a High Street shoe-shop's mark.

We dined together – no one heard the Russians speak more than a 'please' or 'thank you' – and then they disappeared, with Bennett and a chosen retinue. Some time later, when we of the *hoi-poloi*, slouched in the ante-room, had either quite forgotten them or thought them gone, they reappeared amongst us, standing to attention, gloved and hatted, side by side.

The smallest of the group stepped forward, wearing a determined smile. 'Goodnight,' he cried, 'and good luck for landings to the RAF!' He saluted and stepped back among his men, who trooped out like a chorus line, beaming and waving as they went. The episode had been received in total silence, which persisted for some moments after it had passed. Then someone chuckled.

'What an extraordinary thing!'

'Decent of them, really.'

'But hats on in the Mess, old boy. I mean to say…'

'All coked to the gills, of course.'

'Good luck for landings, you chaps!'

Laughter became endemic after that, and for several days we wished each other good luck for landings, on the slightest pretext.

Driving back to Wyton from the evening in the pub at Warboys, the Morris developed symptoms of which Lord Nuffield never dreamed. The headlamps – always rather dimmer than the blackout rules required – now gave no light at all, and our ill-gotten petrol somehow failed to reach the engine, as the guilty thoughts of Hamlet's uncle had refused to rise to heaven. On experiment, we found that Pittam, perched astride the mudguard with the nearside bonnet-cover up, could induce a flow of fuel by exerting pressure with his finger on a small, spring-loaded valve, which he insisted on describing as the carburettor's clitoris. Since his left hand held a torch to light our way, he was inclined to lose his balance when the car turned round a corner. At that, the engine stalled, the light went out, and acrimonious remarks disturbed the silence of the night.

'Why can't you slow down,' he asked, 'going round the bloody bends?'

'I'm trying to, you fool,' I explained. 'The brakes aren't working awfully well.'

'God Almighty! Why can't you get a decent car? This thing's a death-trap.'

'You must ask Nina about that, old sport – she's in charge of the purchasing department. Come on, don't just lie there, crank the dreaded engine.'

'You crank the bastard – I did it last time.'

'You'll do it every bloody time, Sister Hannah. I'm the driver – I have to attend to the controls.'

'Oh, shit!'

Two miles short of Wyton, the nearside front tyre burst. When I pointed out to Pittam that the cause of this was his excessive weight, he descended to profane abuse again. 'Okay,' he said at last, 'let's get the spare on.'

'What spare?'

'Don't tell me you haven't got a spare bloody wheel!'

'Of course I have. What sort of a car do you think this is?

'Right – let's get it on.'

'I said I had a spare wheel. I didn't say it had a tyre.'

More profanity ensued. Eventually, we decided that the tyre and tube were finished anyway, and drove back on the rim, while Pittam made a most unseemly fuss about the permanent damage which he claimed was being occasioned to his spine. When the death-trap had lurched into its parking place and stood there, steaming, with its suspension system creaking back into the rest position, I switched the engine off and, automatically, the lights, which then came on. 'That's good,' I said, 'we've charged the battery up.'

Pittam's conception that I had failed to turn the switch on in the first place was too ridiculous to merit a denial. To ease his mind, however, I denied it anyway. 'The important thing,' I continued, 'is to find another tyre somewhere.'

'And a petrol-pump,' said Pittam, 'and a battery, and some bloody brake-linings.'

Money again. If the love of it was the root of all evil, the lack of it was not much fun, either. The manager of the Westminster Bank's branch in St Ives, to which I had transferred my overdraft, put his finger on it. 'It's an expensive business, maintaining a car,' he said, 'particularly one that may be somewhat past its best. I, myself, could not afford to own one until I was in my fortieth year. Let's see, you are…'

I confessed to being no more than twenty-three.

'Quite so.' He consulted a slip of paper which had been laid before him by a smirking female clerk. 'Your pay and allowances last month totalled thirty-four pounds, eighteen shillings and sixpence. Your withdrawings, on the other hand, were sixty-four pounds, three shillings and one penny.'

I tut-tutted once or twice, to save him the trouble. He was a smaller, greyer, more kindly-looking man than his suburban counterpart in Harrow, but his style was much the same. Wilkins Micawber was alive and well, and working at The Pavement, in St Ives. 'Would I be right,' he asked, 'in thinking that your RAF emoluments represent your sole source of income at the present?'

'I'm afraid so.'

'Hm. My difficulty, you see, is that the Bank's regulations don't allow me to offer you extended credit, on a more or less permanent basis, which is what the present position amounts to – not without some form of security...'

'I can give you a security,' I cried, and told him all about the dear acquaintance of my mother's, until recently a resident of Wimbledon, who had bequeathed to me a great gold watch, complete with chain, of unimaginable value.

'Very nice, I'm sure – but that's not quite what I had in mind...'

What he had in mind was that somebody of substance, known to me, might agree to underwrite the overdraft, against the day the bank decided to change their ink from red to black.

'Is that all you need? That's a piece of cake!' As I spoke, my mind's eye saw a host of fathers, uncles, near and distant cousins, smiling agreeably, substantial to a man. It was true that, when it actually came to writing down their names, the host began to dwindle, back into the mental labyrinths from which they had emerged, until only the hard, familiar core remained. I gave the manager the Whitmore Road address.

'Your father? Splendid. We'll say a limit of £100, shall we? I'll mark your account to that effect.'

It was not the bottomless pool of wealth I had envisaged, but it would serve to clear the overdraft, put the death-trap on the road again, and leave a little over. I cashed a cheque for some of that, and cycled west out of St Ives, along the quiet lanes towards Hemingford Grey and Hemingford Abbotts, twin villages as pleasant as their names, standing by the River Ouse as it drifted through the fields below the airfield. My target was a small hotel, The Grey Hall, in the nearer village, there to spend what time remained of a 36-hour pass with Nina and, inevitably, Pittam. The Grey Hall was run by Mrs Davison, a petite, grey-haired lady of a chic uncommon in East Anglia, assisted by her son and daughter, and in the face of constant efforts by her father-in-law to drink away her profits. Admiration, if not to say unbridled lust, for the elfin daughter, Cherry, gave Pittam his excuse for making up the threesome, but she was far too young and sensible to give him any more than that. His jocular advances when she served us with a splendid lunch (with rich farmland in all directions and an unattached, good-looking woman to do the buying, the rigours of rationing were possible of some amelioration) drew only a polite, automatic giggle in return.

A shower had fallen while we ate, leaving shining patches on the pavement and freshening the air. We walked along the bridle-path to Giddings' boathouse and out on to the landing-stage. Moored below were skiffs, canoes and other sorts of craft.

'Oh, Jack, I'd love a punt,' said Nina. 'Can you manage one?'

'Manage a punt?' I turned to Pittam. 'Did you hear that? She dares to ask me if I can manage a punt!'

'Well, can you?'

'I can manage anything that moves – on land or air or water.'

'Including punts?'

'How do I know until I try?'

While Giddings Senior negotiated terms of hire with Pittam, I took a crash training course with Junior. 'Easy as walking, one leg on the bottom at a time, see? And if the pole gets stuck, just leave hold. Don't try hanging on, 'cause the old punt'll keep going and you'll get wet. There's paddles in the bow if you need 'em.'

Erratically at first, we moved upstream. The water gently slapped the woodwork, and marked our progress with an ever-widening wake. Pittam leaned back in the midships seat, trailing his fingers in the stream. 'Ai-ee-oh-ko,' he boomed, in a brave impersonation of Paul Robeson, 'ai-ee-oh-ko,' with each thrust of the pole.

'The current swings.

The river sings,
A river-rhyme.'

We 'ai-ee-oh-koed' together for a while, and then fell to
chorusing in turn 'The Song of the Volga Boatmen', 'Old
Father Thames' and 'Swanee River'. Moving on from the
particularly riparian to the generally nautical, we went into
the question of what was to be done with the drunken sailor
'earl-eye in the morning'. On the bank, a pair of horses gazed
at us reproachfully across a fence; a disapproving waterhen
led her brood away, in line-astern formation.

'Fourteen days in an open boat,' roared Pittam, 'and
nothing to eat but food: hardships, you bastards? You don't
know what hardships are... Whoops, sorry, Nina!'

But Nina was not listening. She was gazing at a reed-
fringed inlet. 'There's a super place for a bathe,' she said.
'What about it, chaps?'

I had noticed this unhealthy addiction to immersion in
cold water on her part before. 'Not when there's an R in the
month,' I said, firmly, 'thank you very much. Besides, I only
bathe with a Mae West on.'

'I'm game,' cried Pittam, and began unbuttoning his
tunic.

'You fool,' I counselled him, 'that water's freezing!'

'Nonsense,' said Nina, also unbuttoning, 'it'll do you all
the good in the world.'

'It's all right for you,' I said, 'it's a well-known fact that
women have an extra layer of subcutaneous flesh. And if
you think I'm going to be a party to nude bathing, you're
quite mistaken. I'm taking this punt straight back to church
and tell the vicar.

Smugly, Nina revealed the bathing-dress beneath her
uniform; Pittam vowed that he would not remove his
underpants. I pushed the punt's bows in amongst the reeds,
and peered down into the barely-moving water. Several small
fish were moving furtively about their business on the
bottom. 'Don't look to me for help,' I said, 'when you get

into difficulties. I can see the headlines now: "Punting tragedy – two drown…"'

A gleaming shoulder under a cloud of auburn hair moved past me, and Nina hardly made a ripple with her swallow-dive. Pittam's style was more spectacular: holding his nose, and roaring like a maddened bull, he jumped in feet-first, as a man might leave a burning bedroom, trusting to the blanket down below. Almost instantly, he reappeared, still grasping his nose in his right hand, but with the other held above his head, and treading water hard.

'What seems to be the trouble,' I asked, 'have you forgotten how to swim?'

'My wrist-watch,' he howled, bobbing up and down like a cork, 'my bloody Omega – it's not waterproof!'

Waterlogged or not, the Omega was working well enough next night, 17th April, for Pittam to adjust our alarm-clock by. Ten minutes to two was one of those take-off times which gave you the alternative of trying to catch a few hours' sleep before you went, or staying up late and trusting to the oxygen to keep you wakeful through the flight.

We heard the squadrons from the nearby airfields go while we were dressing – 7 from Oakington, 35 from Gravely, 156 from Upwood – but we had lots of time ahead to take a look at Europe's weather, and still make rendezvous with them before they reached their target. This was at a place called Schwandorf, down in south-east Germany, on the edge of the Bavarian Forest, and it was on the list because it was a communications link with the Austrian 'Redoubt' where, so the story went, Hitler's death-or-glory boys would make their final stand.

East Anglia lay dark beneath us as we climbed towards the coast – so dark that it might have been anywhere, or nowhere. Only Pittam's radar recognised that shapeless nothingness for what it was. Those radar blips lit Pittam's world for him, as the cool, blue panel dials lit mine. Outside my cabin window, the exhaust-pipes on the engine's inboard side gave six dancing, yellow flames; beyond the flames was total darkness. If you liked flying in total darkness, this was the time to do it.

We crossed the Essex coast at Clacton and flew south-east for 40 minutes, until Liege was under the port wing; there I turned A-Able easterly, over the Ardennes and on across Koblenz, then swung north-east towards Berlin. It was now almost two hours since I had pulled the wheels up over Wyton, and the darkness, as it always did, had made itself my friend. It gave me little hints to know it better as time passed, nuances to see its character in all the variations from black to not-so-black. There was, as yet, no moon, and high, thin veils of cirrus hid a million stars, but I could sense, if not actually see, where the long curve of the horizon met the sky. Then a flickering of gunfire 30,000 feet below came as a reminder that, down there, the war was going on.

'Any idea where we are, Pip?'

'Coming up to the Harz mountains – why?'

'Just making sure you're on the ball.'

General Bradley's armies, meeting some resistance in those hills, had moved around them (since the fracas over Holland, I had been trying to keep abreast of military affairs): the Ninth going north to take a crack at Magdeburg, the First going south to Halle and to Leipzig. From the further fusillade we saw ten minutes later, it was clear that Magdeburg, for one, was putting up a fight. But the fireworks here, and those around the Harz, were just a prelude to the main event.

I had been to Berlin nine times in the Lancaster, in '43 and '44, and it had never been my favourite target – nor anybody else's, for that matter. Then, there had been mile upon mile of heavy flak and probing searchlights, of malignant, prowling Messerschmitts and ill-intentioned Focke-Wulfes, and of hostile land whichever way you went; now, like a beaten boxer, Berlin was hanging on the ropes, defences down, and taking a terrific pounding from the left and from the right. Butch Harris had once said that they – the

Nazis – sowed the wind, and would reap the whirlwind. Down there, on Able's port beam, that long-awaited harvest was coming home to the Berliners.

The vengeful schoolboy in me thought 'that serves you right, you bastards'; a more sophisticated part of ego knew it for a fearful, cataclysmic sight.

'My God, Pip, just look at that!'

'Uh-huh. Alter course starboard onto one-eight-zero.'

'You see the guns firing from the east – they're Russian, aren't they?'

'Yeah, they would be. Let me know when you're steady on course.'

We flew south across the Elbe, past Dresden on the left and Chemnitz on the right, and on across the Czechoslovak border until we came to Karlsbad, on the starboard beam. There we turned south-west towards Bavaria and the bombers' target. They were to arrive just after five a.m., and I meant to complete the recce thirty minutes earlier, which would give me time to tell the Master Bomber what the weather was while he still had a hundred miles or so to go, although – unless there was a sudden change – I was not going to have a lot to tell.

By now, the night had got to know me well enough to let me see more of its secrets – the total blackness that meant 'forest', and the dull gleam of the Danube as it flowed through Regensburg. If I could see that much from 30,000 feet, the marker crews should have no problem over Schwandorf. There was no need, in that clear sky, to find the cloudbase for the Master Bomber, but a descent would make a change from being six unearthly miles high, and give a chance to take the mask off for a while.

With the Merlins throttled back, and half-flap down to cut the speed, the Mosquito lost height like a falling star. As the darkness of the ground grew big around me, I flicked the mike-switch on. 'What's the highest ground around here, Pip?'

'Nothing much above eight hundred feet – not until the

other side of Nuremberg. Then there's a spot height of sixteen hundred and thirty-three, on track.'

Bavaria went by at 300 mph – woodlands, open fields, a flash of metalled roadway. Perhaps a villager, behind his blackout boards, was wakened by the Merlins' passing roar, and murmured, nestling closer to his wife, 'Don't worry, dear, it's probably one of ours.' In half-an-hour he would be reawakened, and the Lancasters would leave him in no doubt as to whose aircraft they were. I climbed to meet them, leaving Schwandorf to its fate, and kept on climbing, well above their bombing height (once, in a Lancaster myself, I had missed a Mossie, head-on, by the rudders' height – Protheroe had sworn it went between them – and I did not want to startle anyone as I was startled then).

Some 20,000 feet below the bomber force, the US 7th Army were coming south-east too, on their push for Nuremberg. We must have passed above their vanguard somewhere south of Wurzburg, but there was no more sign of them than of the Master Bomber when I called him on the radio at the appointed hour. 'No 1, are you receiving me?' went unanswered – I might as well have called out to the soldiers, or the night.

'Maybe he's got RT trouble,' I conjectured.

'Maybe he's got the chop,' said Pittam. 'Better try the Deputy.'

After two attempts, the Deputy Master Bomber's voice came through against a heavy static background. He said that he was receiving me strength three. In the RT jargon, five was perfect – three was not too bad.

'Here is your weather, No 2,' I said, sharpening my voice and spacing out the words. 'No cloud over target, visibility good, over.'

It seemed a curt conclusion to the rendezvous, and the impulse to say more was strong – to ask the Deputy what sort of trip he had had, to enquire about the welfare of his crew, even to wish him good luck with the marking. I thought quite seriously of offering him the wind that we had found on that part of the route, though I could almost hear his hot-shot navigator snort that he could quite well find his own winds, thank you very much. Then I remembered what I had thought of chatterers when I was flying a bomber, and left the mike switched off.

'Roger, out,' said the Deputy, obviously no gossip, either, and more concerned, perhaps, about where No 1 had gone than he was about the weather.

10,000 feet below A-Able's height, the bombers moved on steadily to Schwandorf, lugging their loads of phosphorescent flares, incendiary and high-explosive bombs, as soundless and unseen to me as Eisenhower's tanks.

An hour or so later, high above the Channel, the first pale light of dawn was in the sky behind us, but we plunged into the night again on the long descent to base. When the wheels touched Wyton's runway, we had been airborne for four hours and a half and covered nearly 1,500 miles. I checked the fuel-gauges: the tanks still held about 150 gallons. It was comforting to know that Able could have stayed up for another 90 minutes if I had needed her to do so. It was even more comforting to know that I did not.

In the next few days, the fate of towns that we had visited that night was changed. Magdeburg, whose garrison had rejected all suggestions of surrender, needed a full Corps assault, supported by a medium bomber group, to bring it down. By 18th April, when the US Ninth moved in, the city was a shambles. The 1st had fought their way through Halle and Leipzig street by street. Within the week Red Army soldiers were looking through their glasses at Berlin.

Meanwhile the Met. Flight aircraft made their sorties – four or five a day – to hunt down all the weather in the European skies. Not the smallest cloud, from the Russian front to the Atlantic, from Norway to the Alps, from MSL to 40,000 feet, was left to live its life in privacy. A blue Mosquito would be sniffing round it, seeking out its secrets, and running home to tell – to Bomber, Fighter, Transport, 2nd TAF and USAF, to anyone who was prepared to listen.

But now the heavy bombers' task was almost done. Berchtesgarten, in the heart of the 'Redoubt' was over-run; oil refineries and aerodromes were coming off the list, for the one could not supply the other with the fuel to fly and fight. The Baltic U-boat bases were to be hit until the end, and Mosquitoes of the Light Night Striking Force would go on peppering Berlin while it was still in German hands. But the time was near when Bomber Harris would call off the dogs. He had always been, to most of us, and would remain, a mighty if a faceless name: the fickle public and their politicians, whose loyalties did not last through changing circumstance, were soon to disavow the very name. Not that he would be – he could not be – dishonoured, but honours were conspicuously not heaped upon him. But then, the Public Executioner was never dubbed Sir Albert Pierrepoint.

Awards, however, came to 1409 Flight. The navigator-adjutant pranced into the crew-room, brandishing a piece of paper. 'Wizard news, you chaps – the CO's got the DFC!'

As the acclamation gradually subsided, he shuffled his feet and hung his head. 'So have I, actually...'

'Whatever for?' I asked.

Pittam's hoot of laughter found no echo in the room.

Russian troops had linked up with the US 1st on 25th April, at Torgau, on the Elbe south of Berlin, but their first contact with the British was at Wismar, in the south-east corner of Lubeck Bay, one week later. Four miles above them, and unaware of the event, I turned back across the Kiel Canal, over Schleswig Holstein, and headed straight for home. Ninety minutes later, I smoked one of Pittam's cigarettes while he dictated from his notes into the telephone. 'Two-tenths cumulus over base, increasing seven-tenths on the coast, decreasing again over most tops at about 19,000 feet. Am I going too fast? Okay. Four-tenths Cu over Denmark and traces of cirrus. The Cu increased to nine-tenths over north-west Germany, with tops to 12,000, and ten-tenths cirrus and isolated cumulo-nimbus…'

It was not the most exciting story he had ever told, but it was all there was to tell of our last mission over Germany. It was enough to send the Light Night Striking Force off happily that night to drop their bombs on Kiel, in what turned out to be the last raid of the war.

We played a cricket match next afternoon, on the field beyond the gardens of the Mess. Wiltshire gave me a grin when I went in to bat, and bowled me a half-volley at a friendly medium pace. This, I promptly drove for four, at which all grinning ceased. A red mist came over his eyes, small horns grew (I could have sworn) on each side of his head, and the next few balls flew past my chest and shoulders like ·5 cannon shells. I was glad to nudge a single, and find refuge at the other end. 'Don't get excited, Wilt,' I said, 'it's only a game.'

'I'll have you, sport, next over,' he panted. 'My bloody oath I will.'

Cricket, after all, was war in miniature, and I was grateful that Australia had been on our side up to then.

On 8th May, Wyton's square was full, from the right flank to the left and front to rear; every officer, airman and airwoman who could stand was on parade. The Station Commander gave the order to 'stand easy', and Air Vice-Marshal Bennett stepped on to the dais. 'Special order of the day, from the Commander-in-Chief.' His voice came through the quickly-rigged loudspeakers, echoing from the surrounding barrack walls.

'Men and women of Bomber Command – more than five-and-a-half years ago, within hours of the declaration of war, Bomber Command first assailed the German enemy. You were then but a handful, inadequate in everything but the skill and determination of the crews for that sombre occasion, and for the unknown years of unceasing battle which lay beyond; black horizons indeed. You, the aircrews, sent your first ton of bombs away on the morrow of the outbreak of war. A million tons of bombs and mines have followed...'

Judging by the sheets of foolscap in his hand, it seemed that the AOC might be going on for quite a while. I wondered whether Nina was listening to Mahaddie giving a similar recital, up the road at Warboys.

'...and you, for long alone, carried the war ever deeper and ever more furiously into the heart of the Third Reich. There the whole might of the German enemy in undivided strength and – scarcely less a foe – the very elements were arrayed against you. You overcame them both...'

Bracing my shoulders, I tried to think of myself carrying things ever more furiously to Germany, but was forced to own that, never particularly furious to start with, I had tended, if anything, to become rather less so as the time went on.

'...you fought alone, as the one force then assailing German soil. You fought as individuals – isolated in your crew stations by the darkness and the murk, and from all other aircraft in company. Not for you the hot emulation of high endeavour in the glare and panoply of martial array. Each crew, each one in each crew, fought alone, through black nights rent only, mile after continuing mile, by the fiercest barrage ever raised, and the instant sally of the searchlights. In each dark minute of those long miles lurked menace. Fog, ice, snow and tempest found you undeterred. In that loneliness in action lay the final test, the ultimate stretch of human staunchness and determination...'

Pittam was wearing his parade-ground expression – like a robot temporarily disconnected from its power-supply. You might have taken him for the very picture of staunchness and determination; of humanity, as well, for you would have noticed that his eyes were fixed three ranks away, where Bunty stood – red-lipped, black-haired, full- breasted – most luscious of the Wyton Waafery.

'...Your losses mounted through those years – years in which your chance of survival through one spell of operational duty was negligible, through two periods, mathematically nil...'

Pittam had been aggrieved that we had barely completed half a tour with 8 Group: I suspected he had secretly aspired to put the ribbon of the DFC beside his DFM.

When I pointed out that Hitler could hardly be expected to keep the war going just for his sake, and consoled him with the thought that we would probably be posted to the Far East, anyway, as Nina had suggested, and that he could slake his thirst for further glory there, he had begun to ruminate upon the physical peculiarities of Oriental women and the quality of beer made out of rice.

'...To you who survive I would say this. Content yourselves, and take credit with those who perished, that now the "cease fire" has sounded, countless homes within our Empire will welcome back a father, a husband or a son whose life, but for your endeavours and your sacrifice, would have been expended during long further years of agony to achieve a victory already ours. No Allied nation is clear of this debt to you. I cannot here expound your full achievements. Your attacks on the industrial centres of Northern Italy did much towards the collapse of the Italians and German armies in North Africa, and to further invasion of the Italian mainland. Of the German enemy, two to three million fit men – potentially vast armies – were continuously held throughout the war in direct and indirect defence against your assaults. A great part of her industrial war effort went to fending off your attacks. You struck a critical proportion of the weapons of war from enemy hands, on every front. You immobilised armies, leaving them shorn of supplies, reinforcements, resources and reserves, the easier prey to our advancing forces...'

Remorselessly (and how else, from that author?), the chronicle continued – of what damage had been done to the enemy's communications, transport, industry and oil, to his Navy and, not least, to his morale. It all sounded like a first-class build-up to a VE-Day party. There would certainly be bonfires, dancing, fireworks, and a most tremendous binge: everyone, on every bomber station, from Middleton to Mildenhall, from Woodhall Spa to Waterbeach, would be coked up to the gills tonight. Everyone, that is, except the few who still had business to attend to, like flying Operation Manna, to drop food supplies to Western Holland, where very little eating had been going on since last November, or Exodus, to bring POWs home from Germany. They might want a weather recce – a crew was needed to stand by. The Adjutant had drawn names from a hat (I should have been more polite about his gong). The aircrews detailed for the mercy-missions would not be getting coked today: nor would Pittam, nor would I.

'...nothing could have been achieved without the devoted service of every man and woman in the Command: those who tended the aircraft, mostly in the open, through six bitter winters, endless intricacies in a prolonged misery of wet and cold, they rightly earned the implicit trust of the crews... those who manned the Stations, Operational Headquarters, supply lines and communications... the pilots of the Photographic Reconnaissance Units, without whose ventures far and wide over enemy territory we should have been largely powerless to plan or strike... the Operational Training organisation which never failed, in the face of every difficulty and unpredicted call, to replace all casualties and to keep our constantly expanding first line up to strength... the men and women of the Meteorological Branch who attained prodigious exactitudes in a fickle art and stood brave on assertion where science is inexact... the meteorological reconnaissance pilots, who flew through anything and everything in search of the feasible...'

Somehow, the words penetrated Pittam's dream of Bunty. He stiffened: the power-supply was reconnected. 'Pilots!' he muttered. 'What about the navigators, for Christ's sake?'

'... the Operational Research sections... the scientists... the Works staffs, the designers... to all of you I would say how proud I am to have served in Bomber Command for 4_ years, and to have been your Commander-in-Chief through more than three years of your saga. Your task in the German war is now completed. Famously have you fought. Well have you deserved of your country and her allies.'

Within the month, many units moved to new locations; some disbanded; crews were parted, just as mine had been in 1944. Cassidy, Protheroe and Walker, all with second tours – or more – completed, would hear or read that Special Order and, as I had thought of them, of Lanham and of Myring too, would think of me. I had survived without them, after all, with Pittam's help. He and I made our farewells, with more than enough East Anglian beer to make up for our dry VE-Day. While he stayed on with 8 Group, I was posted back to Lincolnshire, to test-fly new, white-painted Lancaster Mark VIIs for the squadrons of the Tiger Force, which was to join the USAF in the bombing of Japan. They never would be wanted for that purpose, but we did not know that: we did not know what Robert Oppenheimer knew, that he could make a bomb of which you only needed two to win a war.

Nina's married status brought her quick demobilisation, and a place for us to live was found on Lincoln hill by good, pear-shaped Mr Kirk, who had been permanent (and often honorary) taxi-driver to the crew at Wickenby in 1943. A first-floor room, with use of bath and kitchen, was ours for £2 10s a week, paid in advance. The drive sloped steeply into Nettleham Road, and to start the death-trap in the morning was but to order 'chocks away' and let the force of gravity do the rest. It was a fantasy come true to drive home up the Fosse Way in the evening (remembering to back into the drive), and find a waiting, loving wife, baked beans on toast, and Harris, quietly chewing my slippers by the fire.

With supper done, we were walking further up the hill towards my target for tonight when Nina's fingers tightened on my arm. The great cathedral had come into view, in all its pale stone splendour, between a row of houses and the trees.

'Oh, Jack,' she said, 'that's a lovely sight. And I expect it's beautiful inside, too.'

'I expect it is.'

She halted, smartly, wide eyes staring into mine. 'You haven't been inside?'

I shook my head.

'Don't you think it's time you did?'

'Its still there,' I said, and drew her firmly on towards the Old White Hart. 'That's enough for me.'

GLOSSARY

AFU	Advanced Flying Unit
Air House	The Air Ministry building
Angels	Altitude in thousands of feet, e.g. Angels Five means 5,000 feet
ASI	Air Speed Indicator
ATA	Air Transport Auxiliary
CFI	Chief Flying Instructor
Channel 9	The common RAF radio frequency
CI	Chief Instructor
CO	Commanding Officer
CTO	Chief Technical Officer
Cu	Cumulus cloud
Cypher Queen	A WAAF Code and Cypher Officer
FIS	Flying Instructors School
Form 700	Aircraft Servicing Log
Gee-box	Air-interpreted radar navigation aid, using ground transmissions
G-H	A radar navigational and bombing aid similar to Gee
HE	High Explosive
HCU	Heavy Conversion Unit
IF	Instrument Flying
ITW	Initial Training Wing
LNSF	Light Night Striking Force
'M' Gear	Supercharger set to 'Medium' (cf 'S' Gear - fully super-charged)

MSL	Mean Sea Level
MT	Mechanical Transport
NFT	Night Flying Test
Oboe	As Gee-box, but capable of greater accuracy
OMQ	Officers' Married Quarters
OTU	Operational Training Unit
Oxbox	Airspeed Oxford
PAMPA	Photographic and met recce flight
PFF	Pathfinder Force
P4 Compass	Pilot's magnetic compass
PMC	President of the Mess Committee
PORs	Personnel Occurrence Reports
PR	Photographic Reconnaissance
'P' Staff	Personnel Staff at Headquarters
QFE	Atmospheric pressure at airfield level
QFI	Qualified Flying Instructor
QNH	Atmospheric pressure at MSL, as calculated from QFE
Roger	Message received and understood
RPM	Revolutions per minute
RT	Radio-telephony
SD	Service Dress
SHQ	Station Headquarters
SP	Service Policeman
SROs	Station Routine Orders
TAF	Tactical Air Force
WAAF 'G'	WAAF Officer i/c General Duties
Wilco	I will comply with your instruction
YM	YMCA